D1521543

DISCARD

"Dear Uncle George":

The Correspondence Between Ezra Pound and

Congressman Tinkham of Massachusetts

Photograph of Congressman George Tinkham by
Underwood and Underwood, August 2, 1929.
Reproduced from the Collections of the Library
of Congress.

"Dear Uncle George": The Correspondence Between Ezra Pound and Congressman Tinkham of Massachusetts

Edited by Philip J. Burns

National Poetry Foundation
University of Maine
Orono, Maine 04469-5752

Published by The National Poetry Foundation
University of Maine, Orono, Maine 04469-5752

Printed by Cushing-Malloy, Inc.
Ann Arbor, Michigan

Except for previously copyrighted materials
indicated in acknowledgements and documentation
in the text, all new material is copyright © 1996 by

The National Poetry Foundation
University of Maine
Orono, Maine 04469-5752

Frontispiece and cover photograph of Congressman
George Tinkham by Underwood and Underwood,
August 2, 1929. Reproduced from the Collections of
the Library of Congress.

Library of Congress Number 94-73933
ISBN 0-943373-36-0 (cloth)
0-943373-37-9 (paper)

PS
3531
.O82
Z498
1996

ACKNOWLEDGMENT

For permission to include the complete correspondence of Ezra Pound and George Holden Tinkham and to quote from Bronson Cutting's letter to Pound (24 May 1934), and Pound's letters to F. D. Roosevelt (2 May 1933 and 27 April 1934), W. E. Borah (8 May 1934), and Henry Morgenthau, Sr. (October 1934), acknowledgment is given to the Collection of American Literature, Beinecke Rare Book and Manuscript Library, Yale University.

Grateful acknowledgment is also given to New Directions Publishing Corp. for permission to quote from the following copyrighted works by Ezra Pound: *The Cantos* (Copyright (c) 1934, 1937, 1940, 1948; Copyright (c) 1956, 1959, 1962, 1963, 1966, 1968 by Ezra Pound); *"Ezra Pound Speaking": Radio Speeches of World War II* (Copyright (c) 1978 by The Trustees of the Ezra Pound Literary Property Trust); *Guide to Kulchur* (Copyright (c) 1970 by Ezra Pound); *Pound/Joyce* (Copyright (c) 1967 by Ezra Pound): *Selected Letters* (Copyright (c) 1950 by Ezra Pound); *Selected Prose* (Copyright (c) 1973 by the Estate of Ezra Pound). Quotes from *Jefferson and/or Mussolini* (Copyright (c) 1935, 1936 by Ezra Pound; renewed 1963 by Ezra Pound) are used by permission of Liveright Publishing Company.

Finally, special thanks and acknowledgment are extended to Professor Daniel Pearlman for his sound advice, close reading of the manuscript, perceptive comments, and encouragement.

TABLE OF CONTENTS

NOTE ON THE TEXT

This edition of the correspondence between Ezra Pound and George Holden Tinkham, the United States Representative from the 11th (later the 10th) Massachusetts District from 1915 to 1943 contains all of the extant Pound/Tinkham correspondence, as well as a few letters written to Pound on behalf of the congressman by Tinkham's secretaries, Grace Hamelin and Gertrude Ryan. There are one hundred letters in all, dating from 6 February 1933 until 26 December 1940. The original letters from Tinkham (and his secretaries) to Pound, and the carbon copies of the letters from Pound to Tinkham, are kept at the Beinecke Library at Yale University. The whereabouts of Pound's original letters to Tinkham are unknown.

The introduction to this volume describes the significance of the correspondence and defines its historical, biographical, and rhetorical contexts. Following the annotated text of the letters are two appendixes and a complete bibliography of works cited. Appendix A is an index of all persons mentioned in the letters, and Appendix B is a list of the names of persons mentioned in both the letters and *The Cantos*.

In editing the letters I have used the following conventions:

1. *Arrangement*. The letters are arranged chronologically. In most cases the letters are dated. Where I have had to supply missing dates (usually the year) I have done so on the basis of internal evidence and references to previous letters within the collection.

2. *Missing Passages*. Missing passages are indicated by a series of three asterisks (***).

3. *Crossouts*. Crossouts have been edited according to category as follows:

   a. Crossouts that mark misspellings or typographical errors have been silently removed.

   b. Crossouts that reflect reconsiderations or simple errors in thinking are indicated by enclosing the item in braces ({ }).

c. Crossouts that are indeterminate because the item is totally obscured are indicated by a series of upper case letters, the same ones Pound used to obscure the item (e.g., HHHHH).

4. *False Starts*. False starts (where Pound mistyped a word, then typed it correctly but neglected to cross out the error) have been silently eliminated.

5. *Misspellings*. Pound's playful or otherwise intentional misspellings have been retained, but those that are clearly unintended or that result from typographical errors have been silently corrected. Misspellings whose cause is indeterminate have been retained, but the Latin marker *sic* is inserted in square brackets immediately following the word.

6. *Upper/Lower Case Inconsistencies*. Pound's inconsistent capitalization of proper names relating to nationalities (e.g. British vs. british) has been retained. However, with regard to Pound's habit of using lower case letters at the beginning of some sentences, case has been determined according to the following principle: if the sentence may be interpreted as an afterthought in relation to the previous sentence, thereby rendering the first period problematical, the lower case letter has been retained; on the other hand, if the second sentence bears no such relationship to the first, the initial lower case letter has been silently changed to a capital.

7. *Punctuation*. Punctuation has not been altered except where Pound neglects to supply closing parentheses and, in one case, a closing quotation mark. In each circumstance, the righthand parenthesis or quotation mark has been silently inserted using editorial judgment. Pound's idiosyncratic use of the slanted line (/) in place of conventional punctuation has been emulated because, in many cases, it would be too difficult, if not impossible, to determine which conventional mark would be appropriate.

8. *Emphasis*. Pound's use of capital letters for emphasis has been emulated.

9. *Typography*. Pound's use of the "equals" sign in place of the hyphen and his use of the upper case I in place of the Arabic numeral 1 have been emulated. While these substitutions may have been dictated by mechanical or keyboard limitations of Pound's typewriter, they nonetheless contribute to the peculiar character of the letters and, for that reason, should be retained.

10. *Editorial Insertions*. My editorial comments, of which there are few, are indicated by square brackets ([ ]). Also, in letters where I have had to insert part of the date (usually the year), I have enclosed my insertion in square brackets ([ ]).

11. *Annotations*. To make the notes more accessible to the reader, they have been placed immediately following the particular letters with which they are associated.

INTRODUCTION

Ezra Pound's prolific letter-writing has been well documented in numerous Pound biographies, and many of his letters have been published in book form. The *Selected Letters*, published in 1950, is probably the most familiar volume, but there are additional volumes devoted to his correspondence with specific individuals as well. These individual volumes include Pound's correspondence with his wife-to-be, Dorothy Shakespear; his sometime mentor, Joseph Darling ("Bib") Ibbotson; one of his proteges, John Theobald; as well as more famous people such as James Joyce and Wyndham Lewis. The available letters, however, despite their great number, represent merely the tip of the iceberg of the complete Pound correspondence, most of which still resides at university libraries, particularly those at Indiana University, Yale University, and the University of Texas at Austin. Nor does the published correspondence provide a true cross-section of Pound's letters. While the published letters do include correspondence with a diversity of individuals and cover most of Pound's favorite themes, they do not include a body of letters that could be clearly identified as "political correspondence." Indeed, what is missing from the *Selected Letters* and from the other volumes is Pound's correspondence with politicians and other public officials who were in a position to influence public policy. As a result, the published letters omit a sustained, focused discussion of politics and economics, an omission that is striking because of Pound's well-documented political concerns and his obsession with economics.

The omission is even more striking because Pound did carry on a voluminous correspondence with public officials, especially those who were part of or who held office during Roosevelt's New Deal Administration (Pearlman 419; Walkiewicz and Witemeyer 441). Of this large political segment of Pound's letter-writing, his "three most sustained correspondences" were with Senator William Borah of Idaho, Senator Bronson Cutting of New Mexico, and Representative George H. Tinkham of Massachusetts – all Republicans with whom Pound felt an emotional and philosophical affinity (Pearlman 419-20).

Although Senators Borah and Cutting were doubtlessly more important than Tinkham in terms of national politics, the Massachusetts Congressman was not a complete unknown. In 1930, during a session of Senator Caraway's lobby investigating committee, he entered the national limelight by delivering an eloquent speech attacking two influential church organizations, the Board of Temperance, Prohibition and Public Morals of the Methodist Episcopal Church, and the Federal Council of the Churches of Christ in America (McKee 298). Moreover, his name resurfaced from time to time thereafter, usually in connection with speeches or other statements he would release to the press against one or another of his "great hatreds," which included, among others, virtually any form of internationalism (not the least of which was international finance), pacifism, Roosevelt and the New Deal, as well as violations of the principle of separation of church and state (McKee 304; "Tinkham, George H[olden]" 838). However, apart from his red beard, which was universally acknowledged as the most impressive in Congress, and his collection of African game trophies and other exotic items that filled his Washington apartment ("one of the most bizarre places in the city") (McKee 304), these intermittent attacks comprised his only basis for a national reputation. Expending precious little energy on the daily affairs of Congress and being a signatory to no significant legislation of national scope, he preferred to minister to the wants of his Boston constituents – a task to which he applied himself and the resources of his office with extreme diligence. For the rest, he spent his time gathering vast stores of information that would support his political philosophy and supply ammunition for his eloquent harangues. He was therefore regarded by many as an effective Congressman within the domain of his constituency on the one hand, and a knight errant tilting at straw dragons on the other (McKee 301-04; "Tinkham, George H[olden]" 838).

Despite his lack of national stature, Tinkham's correspondence with Pound is more important than the correspondence of Borah and Cutting in terms of quantity and reciprocity. It is more extensive than the Borah correspondence by three-to-one, in addition to being more reciprocal, Borah having written only "three brief replies"; and the Cutting correspondence was cut short by the Senator's untimely death in 1935 (Pearlman 419-20). Apart from quantity and reciprocity, moreover, the Pound-Tinkham letters are valuable in their own right. Extending from February 1933 through the 1940 national elections, thus spanning most of the turbulent 1930s with its world economic and political crises culminating in the Second World

War, Pound's letters to the Massachusetts Congressman concentrate on many of the poet's economic and political ideas that are dispersed throughout the poetry of *The Cantos* and expressed variously in prose works such as *ABC of Economics* (1933), *Jefferson and/or Mussolini* (1935), and *Guide to Kulchur* (1938). Moreover, the letters refer candidly, and in many cases repeatedly, to more than 300 personalities and events, the overwhelming majority of which are referred to in Pound's literary texts. More than 20% of these references appear in *The Cantos* alone. Since Pound's poetry and published prose are so highly allusive and yet restricted to a limited number of characteristic themes, and since Pound's correspondence with Tinkham addresses some of the more important themes and shares many of the allusions, the letters can serve as a suggestive commentary on or companion to the literature.

In addition, the letters show Pound in an interesting rhetorical position. Writing to a United States Congressman whom he perceives as right-thinking on important issues, Pound's self-appointed role is neither to criticize nor to convert, but to inform, encourage, and assist. We see in these letters not just the impassioned lecturer or cantankerous gadfly, but a political advisor, strategist, and would-be aide, who offers his services out of a developing friendship, a common philosophy, and a desire to put this philosophy into action at the highest levels of national government. This is not to say that elements of the more familiar Pound do not pervade these letters – indeed, they are clearly and abundantly there. But Pound the lecturer and social critic, the venter of spleen and opinion, and even the self-acknowledged Great Man are subordinate to Pound the citizen-in-absentia, the eccentric patriot bent on action, the intellectual in the (hypothetical) caucus room. Apart from extending (or refining) our already multiple perspectives on Pound, the consistent rhetorical stance he assumes in these letters is important because it helps to explain, though not to excuse, later events in his life, notably his Rome Radio speeches and subsequent indictment for treason – and this despite the wrongheadedness and meanspiritedness of some of his ideas and comments in many of the letters themselves.

What has been said thus far is intended to explain the need for the present volume of letters: in sum, I have argued that the Pound-Tinkham correspondence will begin to fill the political gap in the available Pound letters as well as contribute to Pound studies in general. What follows is a series of contexts – historical, biographical, and rhetorical – that are presented as a threefold approach to situate and understand the letters and their production.

THE HISTORICAL CONTEXT

The 1930s was a climactic decade for the Western democracies and for America in particular. Beginning with the economic collapse of a capitalism gone haywire, the worldwide depression was a time of political upheaval and social and economic chaos in which the material and spiritual needs of Europeans were held hostage to presumably irreconcilable ideologies rather than met by effective policy. As Arthur M. Schlesinger, Jr., has pointed out, the prevailing viewpoint in Europe held that a state-directed economy was wholly inconsistent with capitalism. There could be no middle ground, no socially directed capitalism, so the choices were either/or: either "parliamentary democracy with economic chaos" or "economic authoritarianism with political tyranny" (98). The more willful choice was the latter, and by 1933 it had long been made in Soviet Russia, Germany, and Italy, where the totalitarian option had already produced the Communist, Nazi, and, most pertinent to Ezra Pound, Fascist states. The democratic option was less a choice than a failure to choose, for the liberal governments in countries such as Great Britain and France, especially at the beginning of the decade, opted for little more than the status quo. Seeing no middle-ground possibility and refusing to commit themselves to complete socialism, "they had no alternative but to accept the logic of laissez-faire" and somehow survive the crisis (100).

The great exception to these alternatives – totalitarianism on the Right and Left versus the ineffectual coexistence of liberal-socialist sentiment and laissez-faire capitalism – was the American experiment of Franklin Roosevelt's Administration. The virtues of the New Deal – the hope that it inspired as well as its accomplishments – derived from its ability to implement practical measures that pulled in the reins of an irresponsible capitalism on the one hand, and to remain free of the constraints of ideological purism on the other. Moreover, it did so without shocking the American system. The New Deal did not constitute a revolutionary change in American life, a cataclysmic shift in response to economic collapse; rather, it responded to the collapse and the subsequent Great Depression in an evolutionary way. It brought to fruition various developments stemming from widespread unrest among diverse groups, including labor, farmers, intellectuals. and ethnic minorities – developments that had been gathering momentum beneath the facade of national prosperity (95-97). The "liberal pragmatist *par excellence*," Roosevelt used what was at hand from the American liberal-capitalist tradition, along with some new ideas from Keynesian economics (e.g., emphasis on government spending and public works) to forge new and effective policies that revitalized the national social and economic health within the constraints of a sometimes strained but ultimately flexible Constitution (103-04).

Keynes himself perceived the boldness of Roosevelt's program, praising its promise, though not without noting its risks. Schlesinger quotes Keynes from an open letter to the President, written in 1933:

> You have made yourself the trustee for those in every country who seek to mend the evils of our condition by reasoned experiment within the framework of the existing social system. If you fail, rational choice will be gravely prejudiced throughout the world, leaving orthodoxy and revolution to fight it out. But, if you succeed, new and bolder methods will be tried everywhere, and we may date the first chapter of a new economic era from your accession to office. (104)

Keynes was not alone in the tone of his early perceptions of the New Deal. Ezra Pound, too, saw both promise and risks in Roosevelt's "accession," although he would articulate them differently than Keynes, and although, unlike Keynes (for whom he had no use, calling him a "blathering trained seal" in Letter 15), he would quickly shift from proponent to severe critic. A glance at where Pound stood in the course of his life and thought by the early 1930s should help to explain what underlay those views in general and the Tinkham letters in particular.

VORTEX RAPALLO AND
THE ANTI-ROOSEVELT CAMPAIGN

When Pound moved to Rapallo in 1924, it marked the third in a series of self-imposed "exiles" that had begun more than a decade earlier. Having visited London briefly in 1906 and having lived there from 1908 to 1910, Pound returned in earnest in 1911 (Stock, *Life* 29, 53-96). For him life in the United States had been intellectually, artistically, and spiritually barren. New York, according to Michael Reck's account, was "too provincial" for Pound, and "American poetry was almost nonexistent" (18). London, however, "was Pound's Mecca" (11), and during his long sojourn there he centered himself in circles of intellectual and artistic vitality. The First World War put an end to that, however, and in 1921, "fed up with England" (39), he moved to Paris. Immersed in "the magical Paris ambiance" (40), Pound regained his intellectual and creative energies, but after four years he "again felt that he had come to a dead end" (48). By 1924 he had grown tired of Paris, especially the whirl of its social life, and he had come to regard Paris itself as "tired" (49). Moreover, he felt that "the important things were happening elsewhere." Having discovered on recent visits to Mussolini's Italy that conditions there were conducive to his needs, he moved on to Rapallo, where he would remain for the next twenty years (Stock, *Life* 256).

To trace the moves in Pound's exile is to follow the stages of a quest. From his "barren" homeland to the intellectual vitality of London, from a London "in terror of thought" (Pound, quoted in Reck 48) to artistic Paris, and from "tired" Paris to the new Italy, Pound continually sought out a vital center of intellectual, artistic, and spiritual activity –what he would call a "vortex"–that could sustain him in his various endeavors and, by extension, the culture at large. Clearly, it was not until he settled in Italy that his vortex became more or less stable, despite the ironic fact that in Rapallo, in contrast to London and Paris, he lived in far less proximity to the other artists, intellectuals, and others on whom the vortex depended. As a result he had to import his circle of friends and proteges (not too difficult a task since, as James Laughlin points out, "the trains from Paris to Rome all stop in Rapallo" [9]); and what is more to the point, he had to write letters. In a very real sense, "the Rapallo vortex" funneled through the mail.

While Pound was undertaking the progressive stages of his exile, his thinking about economics was undergoing a not altogether unrelated development. When the philosopher-poet T. F. Hulme, and the sculptor Henri Gaudier-Brzeska, both friends of Pound, were killed in the trenches in the First World War, Pound interpreted the loss as youth and talent sacrificed to the interests of munitions makers and international bankers who profited from the War. Their deaths, and those of others like them, left a void that for Pound was filled with a hellish vision of postwar England:

> Profiteers drinking blood sweetened with sh-t,
> And behind them ...... f and the financiers
> lashing them with steel wires. (14/61)

This vision, in addition to spurring his move to Paris, was probably as important as any other factor in turning his mind increasingly to economics (Laughlin 152), particularly the economics of war and the economics of want. His inquiries into the subject convinced him that wars are created to make markets for war materiel, thereby filling the pockets of profiteers and bankers, and that the cause of want was not a deficiency of production but of distribution. While both of these observations led to his obsessive attacks on international financiers, who, he believed, conspired to keep money out of circulation so that they could grow fat on usurious rates of interest, these attacks were balanced by the more positive side of his economics. This constructive side stressed a rethinking of the nature of money, particularly as a mode of circulation of goods and services, the production of which, in the industrialized world, was or need not be a serious problem. This emphasis on circulation placed the onus on the distribution of money: as Pound saw it, the primary economic need was to increase the purchasing power of the average person.

Crucial to his thinking along these lines were the ideas of "Major" C. H. Douglas, a civil engineer and economic theorist, whom Pound "discovered" under the auspices of A. R. Orage at the *New Age* in 1918 (Laughlin 153). Douglas' theory of Social Credit held that the problem of purchasing power could be solved by means of a "National Dividend," a monetary sum to which all citizens except the very rich were entitled by virtue of the "Cultural Heritage," which included the productive capacity of the nation as well as nature's bounty (Finlay 112). As Pound studied economics throughout the 1920s and into the 1930s, seeking always to gain converts to Social Credit, his thinking did not adhere to pure Douglasism, but rather combined other ideas with a Social Credit essence. In Laughlin's phrase, "Pound may have been the inventor, intellectually at least, of the Cuisinart. He kept pouring new ingredients into the ever-protesting gullet of Major Douglas" (153). These "ingredients" included economic ideas from an otherwise heterogenous group of sources, many of which, such as the following, are mentioned in his letters to Tinkham: the history of the Monte dei Paschi bank in Siena, Thomas Jefferson, John Adams, Andrew Jackson, Martin Van Buren, McNair Wilson, Christopher Hollis, Montgomery Butchart, Francis Delaisi, Peter Larranaga, Willis Overholser, Odon Por, W. E. Woodward, Jerry Voorhis, Dexter Kimball, Henry Ford, Confucius, Mencius, Fascist corporatism, and Pound's own grandfather, Thaddeus Coleman Pound.

The most important "additive" to Pound's version of Social Credit was *Schwundgeld*, or stamp scrip, which was invented by a relatively obscure German economist, Silvio Gesell, and had been employed with temporary success in the small Austrian town of Woergl. Because it required that the bearer periodically affix a postage stamp to keep it valid, stamp scrip was "a self-liquidating currency that would discourage hoarding" (Laughlin 158). It therefore squarely addressed the question of circulation, which nicely complemented Social Credit's emphasis on distribution.

By the 1930s Pound's "Cuisinart" had produced a blend of economic thinking that was virtually complete; his ideas had matured to the extent that he considered himself a genuine economist, and he presented himself as such to the world in both his public writing and his private correspondence. Moreover, he had come to believe that the world, if properly educated about the nature of its economic problems, would adopt the practical solutions offered by his version of Social Credit. This perception was no doubt conditioned by his vantage point in Rapallo. Living in Fascist Italy, he approved of the social and economic policies that Mussolini had implemented. Indeed, as Earl Davis suggests, Pound admired Mussolini's version of government control and his encouragement of a national economy, considering them favorably in terms of his own ideal of Confucian order (128, 136). In addition, he thought Italian corporatism provided "an ideal social basis for the implementation of Social Credit" (Laughlin 162).

What is more important is that Pound *believed* in Mussolini—a belief that is crucial to understanding Pound's embrace of Fascism. Writing *Jefferson and/or Mussolini* in 1933 (at the same time that he was beginning his correspondence with Congressman Tinkham), Pound addresses this notion of belief:

> Any thorough judgment of MUSSOLINI will be in a measure an
> act of faith, it will depend on what you *believe* the man means,
> what you believe he wants to accomplish. (33, Pound's emphasis)

What Pound believed Mussolini wanted to accomplish, moreover, was something that, in his estimation, boded well for a new economic era in America. The dominant theme of *Jefferson and/or Mussolini*, which follows a strange and idiosyncratic logic, to be sure, is that Mussolini embodied the Jeffersonian spirit that had dominated American thinking, particularly in the realm of economics, up until the end of the Van Buren administration, after which it had been suppressed by private financial interests. Mussolini's Fascist State, in other words, was a twentieth-century reenactment, Italian style, of Jeffersonian America! More to the point, Pound's observation implied that if the United States would adopt certain economic ideas, and if her leadership would exhibit a Mussolinian constructive will, and if she could adapt these ideas and this type of leadership to her local conditions and democratic traditions, then Jeffersonian America would thrive once again. America would thus regain her rightful course, which had been abandoned after Van Buren.

These developments in Pound's life and thought – his progressive exile, his economics, and his belief in Mussolini – had come to a head in 1933 when Roosevelt took office. Convinced that a "new order" was at hand in Italy and could be realized in America, Pound naturally focused much of his attention on the new President and his administration. At first he was optimistic, and he said so. In January 1934 he declares himself "a supporter of, and hoper for the [Roosevelt] administration," but in the same breath his optimism begins to wane – something about "dear Frankie" communicating with "british private swindling interests" ("Current Hopes").

This qualified optimism had much to do with his perceptions of the preceding administrations. To Pound, Wilson was "a man incapable of receiving ideas . . . a type of low vitality" ("This Super Neutrality"), and he called the terms of Harding, Coolidge, and Hoover a "period of infamy...[when] America was largely acephalous" (*Kulchur* 132). Nor was he always so polite, referring to "the filth of american govt. through the reigns of Wilson, Harding, Coolidge and the supremely uncultivated, uneducated gross Hoover. . ." (*Kulchur* 155-56). Therefore, in June 1935, when Pound writes in *The New English Weekly* that he has "no superlative hopes" for the Roosevelt administration, it is no surprise when he adds that "it is immeasurably superior to what the U. S. wished on itself with Wilson, Harding, Coolidge and Hoover." But the most telling comment from the same article is that Roosevelt's administration "has come so near to being a good administration, yet is not" ("American Notes," 7 [1935]: 205).

A letter Pound wrote to the President on 2 May 1933, less than two months after Roosevelt's inauguration, contains a clue to what he may have meant by "has come so near. . . ." Praising him for his book, *Looking Forward*, which had just been published, Pound writes that he has recommended the book to the readers of the Paris edition of the *Chicago Tribune*, and he cites page 128 as the book's "highwater mark." Page 128 contains the following paragraph:

> Our economic life today is a seamless web. Whatever our voca-
> tion, we are forced to recognize that while we have enough facto-
> ries and enough machines in the United States to supply all our
> needs, these factories will be closed part of the time and the
> machines will lie idle if the buying power of fifty million people
> remains restricted or dead.

With this emphasis on the problem of monetary distribution,
Pound must have concluded that the President shared his concerns. At any rate, in the letter he goes on to mention his own
Jefferson and/or Mussolini, and says it was "written in Feb. from
motives which seem very to me like those which moved you to
write yr/ own bok [sic]." He then proceeds, in true Poundian
fashion, to suggest that the President read C. H. Douglas and
(because the Roosevelt passage quoted above is embedded in a
chapter on agriculture) advises him to apply "what you say of
[the farmer's part] of the nation's purchasing power to the purchasing power of the WHOLE NATION, in relation to the
whole nation's product." Then he concludes: "The distance from
there to Douglas's main theorem seems to me fairly short."

Early on, then, it is clear that Pound regarded the
Roosevelt administration as having the potential to implement
sound economic measures, and seven months into the New Deal
he was still keeping the faith. In a *New Democracy* article of 25
August 1933, he portrays Roosevelt as something of a knight
among knaves: Roosevelt, he says, "has introduced a new terminology and several new concepts into the circle of scoundrels
and cannon feeders, pimps assembled in London calling itself an
Economic Conference" ("Points"). Although Pound does not
specify the particulars of Roosevelt's "new terminology" and
"new concepts," he may have been referring to the following
passage from Roosevelt's wireless to the Conference on 3 July
1933 – a passage that is not inconsistent with Poundian economics:

> The sound internal economic system of a Nation is a greater factor
> in its well-being than the price of its currency in changing terms of
> the currencies of other Nations. It is for this reason that reduced
> cost of Government, adequate Government income, and ability to
> service Government debts are all so important to ultimate stabil-
> ity. So too, old fetishes of so-called international bankers are being
> replaced by efforts to plan national currencies with the objective
> of giving to those currencies a continuing purchasing power which
> does not greatly vary in terms of the commodities and needs of
> modern civilization. Let me be frank in saying that the United
> States seeks the kind of dollar which a generation hence will have
> the same purchasing and debt-paying power as the dollar value we

hope to attain in the near future. . . . (Roosevelt, *Public Papers* 264-65)

Even though Pound's "hope" for the New Deal was waning by January 1934, he was not to abandon it altogether until some years later. On 27 April 1934 he again wrote to the President, this time to call his attention to an obvious misprint in his recently published *On Our Way*. In addition to pointing out the error, he explains, somewhat curiously, "I am reviewing [the book] with what temperance my conscience permits and with considerably [*sic*] doubt as to my criticism passing the printer," and closes with this equally curious sentiment: "With best wishes and...convictions that you have not publicly shared" (Pound's ellipsis). The curiosity is twofold: on the one hand Pound suggests that he disapproves (vehemently, one might suppose) of what Roosevelt has written, but on the other hand he implies that the book does not express Roosevelt's true convictions. The letter reveals Pound's hope even as it conceals it, for in this case the President's "convictions" constitute Pound's hope for the administration, even though they remain unexpressed. It is a problem that became thematic with Pound as he grew more critical of the New Deal and its leaders. On the basis of his reading of *Looking Forward*, he suspected that Roosevelt understood the basic economic problem of distribution and purchasing power, and he believed that Roosevelt was aware of the answer to the problem (Pound, "Mr. Roosevelt at the Crossroads"), so he harbored a diminishing faith in the President that lingered throughout the first term of his administration. But it was never more than the palest shade of optimism:

> AT LAST the President has made a very astute speech at Atlanta. AT LAST, after three years social credit hammering Great White Father has TOLD his flock that Americans are LIVING on a THIRD CLASS DIET. For the very simple reason that the masses of the American people have not the purchasing power to eat more and better food.... The Atlanta speech is a high tribute to the achievements of the administration...BUT Roosevelt still offers the false dilemma between England's dirty old clothes, the dole, degrading and dishonoring, and Public Works on the Italian Model. ("American Notes," 8 [1936]: 265)

a glimmer of potential:

> Increasing evidence that Roosevelt, personally, has an inkling of America's NEED for Social Credit (whatever he may think is practical politics on a given day).("American Notes," 8 [1936]: 465)

or a sardonic comment:

> A roseate whisper has reached us that F. D. R. has murmured
> something about "reversal of interest," that is...a drift toward the
> Gesellite system to be applied somewhere in the interstices of
> Morgenthau's "department!" ("Bravo Roosevelt!")

By the end of Roosevelt's first term, Pound's hopes
for the administration, far from being "superlative," had played
out their slow death. From then on there was nothing left to
temper his attack.

Pound's case against the Roosevelt administration
can be divided into four principal issues, as described below.

1. Pound's attitude toward the New Deal was tied to
his contempt for the international banking system, or the
"usurocracy," as he called it. In his view, international finance
was a swindle because it profited, without being productive, at
the expense of the people of a nation. He explains "the trick" as
follows:

> Whenever the Rothschild and other gents in the gold business
> have gold to sell, they raise the price. The public is fooled by pro-
> pagandising the devaluation of the dollar, or other monetary unit
> according to the country chosen to be victimised. The argument is
> that the high price of the monetary unit is injurious to the nation's
> commerce. But when the nation, that is, the people of that nation,
> own the gold and the financiers own the dollars or other monetary
> units, the gold standard is restored. This raises the value of the
> dollar and the citizens of "rich" nations, as well as citizens of other
> nations, are diddled. ("An Introduction" 181)

Pound's opposition to Roosevelt and his administration can be
measured by the extent to which they were, in Pound's estimation, influenced by or in league with the international financiers.

2. Pound thought the New Deal enslaved the people
through economic policies that kept them in debt to private
interests. "Usury," he said, "is an instrument for increasing debt,
and for keeping the debtor in debt perpetually or at least for the
longest possible period. And it is hypocrisy to prattle of liberty
unless the liberty includes the freedom to keep out of debt"
("To Recapitulate" 261). True liberty for Pound would result
from a non-usurious policy that would solve the problem of distribution. Only then would the people be free of the enslavement and humiliation of the dole, which in his view was
"incitement to shiftlessness with concurrent PENALIZATION
of everyone who is efficient or willing to be" (Letter 15).

3. Pound thought Roosevelt had violated his oath to
uphold the Constitution and was therefore guilty of perjury.
Moreover, by handing over the nation's money to the financiers
in violation of the Constitution's provision for state control of

the supply and value of money, Roosevelt, according to Pound, was guilty of embezzlement. Pound considered these transgressions treasonous and thought the President should be brought to justice because of them. As Pound explains it,

> SOVEREIGNTY inheres in the right to issue money, and the American sovereignty belongs by LAW to the people, and their representatives in CONGRESS have the right to issue money and to determine the value thereof. And one hundred and twenty MILLION suckers have lamentably failed to insist on the observation of this "DECIDED law," . . . . The point at which embezzlement of the nation's funds on the part of her officers becomes treason can be decided only by jurists, and not by hand picked JUDGES hired to support illegality. ("Indecision" 84)

    4. Based on his belief in the theory that wars are caused intentionally by the "usurocracy," Pound thought Roosevelt, through his connections with international finance, was leading the country into another world war, and this too he considered criminal.

    These four interrelated issues were the key ones in Pound's criticism of Roosevelt. All of them reducing to a single term – economics – they became the theme of an attack.

    Pound carried out his campaign against Roosevelt chiefly through articles in *New Democracy* during the first years of the New Deal, in *The New English Weekly* beginning in 1934, and via the Rome Radio broadcasts during the war. He gives an early hint of what was to come in a *New Democracy* article of June 1934, entitled "Mr. Roosevelt at the Crossroads":

> The answer to the present trouble is known. The president knows it is known, and has SAID so (March 4th). Whether he chooses to betray the people and continue the Hoover system of handing the increase of purchasing power to particular cliques, groups, grafters, or to give it to the people per capita is the issue. It is Roosevelt's particular problem; and by it he will be blessed or damned.

    If the fate of Roosevelt's soul was hanging in the balance in June 1934, Pound saw which way the scales had tipped by July. In *The New English Weekly* he writes:

> It is an infamy that the STATE in, and by reason of, the very act of creating material wealth should run into debt to individuals. It is on this evil that Franklin Roosevelt is headed plumb bang to hell, and all liberal shysters with him. ("Ecclesiastical History" 273)

    By January 1935 Pound's critical view of Roosevelt and his administration had all but solidified. Despite the lingering hopes mentioned above, his characteristic posture was now one of attack, and his theme the perceived connection between Roosevelt, international finance, and the Jews:

> Roosevelt gets no help from his entourage. There is no one among his advisers who can, or who, presumably, would have the patience or courage to tell him anything he doesn't already know. The only constant pull is from the Lehman, Richberg contingent .... There is positively no evidence against Roosevelt's being utterly under the thumb of international finance. ("American Notes," 6 [1935]: 270)

It was about mid-1935 that Pound's anti-semitism became more closely linked with his attitude toward Roosevelt. Whereas previously it had been present in his references to the President's associates (the "liberal shysters," the "Lehman. Richberg contingent") and thereby applied to Roosevelt by association, it now began to merge with his conception of the President himself. Writing in *The New English Weekly* in July 1935, Pound says:

> It is not so much that Frank Roose(n)velt has cooperated with the Levys as that their cousins the Lehmanns, Baruchs, Morgensteins, etc. have cooperated him [*sic*]. Roosevelt is fundamentally the usurers' champion. ("American Notes," 7 [1935]: 225)

By Hebraicizing the President's name (a practice that would become habitual–and more extreme–with Pound), Pound seemed to have transformed the man into a symbol of what he found contemptible in the New-Deal-World-Usurocracy complex. And by transporting Roosevelt to the level of symbol, thereby dehumanizing him, Pound seemed to have unleashed the baser elements of his own criticism. These elements received their fullest (and most vile) expression in the wartime radio broadcasts. Consider the following excerpts, taken more or less at random:

> . . . that any sub-Jew in the White House should send American lads to die for their Jewsoons and Sassoons and the private interest of the scum of the English earth . . . ("Power," 19 February 1942)

> If Roosevelt were not BELOW the biological level at which the concept of honor ENTERS the mind...that liar would... commit hara-kiri .... Frankie Finklestein Roosevelt. ("The Pattern," 30 March 1942)

> [Roosevelt's] set of Kikettes .... ("Indecision," 9 April 1942)

> President is an imbecile...dumb cluck, a goof...two-fisted double-time liar...Franklin D. Frankfurter Jewsfield .... ("More Homely," 18 February 1943)

Judeocracy...new Jerusalem, the new Jew Roosevelt oosalem. ("Serviti," 21 February 1943)

...the Kikefurter, Morgenberg, Cohen, and company administration. ("Pots to Fracture," 9 March 1943)

The list could be extended, but the drift should be more than apparent without adding to the string of epithets. If the print medium had exerted any control at all over the nature of Pound's invective, no such restraint was imposed by the airwaves. Through the Italian microphone Pound spit forth his venom, but the spitting forth was more a purging, serving more to flush out his accumulating hatred and frustration than to influence his listeners in any constructive way.

In any case, his more coherent attack was still to find voice in print. As late as 1944 Pound had not abandoned the field. In his pamphlet, *America, Roosevelt and the Causes of the Present War*, he outlines the theory that wars "are provoked in succession, deliberately, by the great usurers, in order to create debts, ... so that they can extort the interest on these debts ...." and he describes Roosevelt's role in this diabolical scheme:

> Roosevelt being in all this a kind of malignant tumor, not autonomous, not self-created, but an unclean exponent of something less circumscribed than his own evil personal existence; a magistrate with *legally* limited jurisdiciton, a perjurer, not fully aware of what he does, why he does it, or where it leads to. His political life ought to be brought *sub judice*. (18)

This characterization of Roosevelt, even though it is hardly less obscene than the broadcasts, reveals a mind in control of its discourse. More than that, it focuses not only the sentiment, but the theme as well as the intent of the ten years' war Pound waged, one might say unilaterally, against the President.

Pound's campaign against Roosevelt throughout the President's four administrations is crucial to an understanding of his political correspondence in general and his letters to Tinkham in particular. The President, members of his cabinet, his advisors, and his activities and policies gave concrete form to many of the abstractions that were anathema to Pound, and being concrete they provided real enemies that Pound could fight in the real world. Whereas all of his writing, including *The Cantos*, his published prose, and his other correspondence, waged a verbal battle against nefarious ideology, disembodied or otherwise, his political correspondence served that purpose and more. Because of its particular audience and rhetorical aims, it could stimulate immediate and practical change at the sources of power through votes, Congressional activities, and political campaigns. His political correspondence therefore became a potential means of putting his ideas into action, the most direct means he could use from Rapallo.

THE RHETORICAL CONTEXT

While Pound's political letter-writing, as it turned out, did not succeed in bringing about the political and economic changes that he sought, the effort was nevertheless successful in achieving lesser rhetorical aims.

One of these aims was consistent with a dominant aim of his correspondence in general: writing from Rapallo Pound wanted to establish a network of intelligent people, a "chosen six hundred" who would form the core of an enlightened civilization. He was always on the lookout for "a special intelligence," and when he found one, whether it be in a book or magazine or through some other medium, he would initiate a correspondence with the individual and try to put that person in touch with like-minded others (Laughlin 42). In the case of Tinkham, a Congressional speech attacking the Carnegie Endowment provided the impetus.

Writing to Tinkham on 6 February 1933 (Letter 1), Pound opens on a strong congratulatory note: "AND CHEERS!! Damn well time someone said so ...." And so begins the correspondence that would last until the war, which effectively cut him off from not only Tinkham, but most of his other American communicants as well. As he would complain over Rome radio:

> ... I write letters to and read letters from the most intelligent of my contemporaries, and Mr. Churchill and that brute Rosefield, and their kike postal spies and obstructors...annoy me by cuttin' off my normal mental intercourse with my colleagues. ("Books and Music" 7)

Despite its abrupt termination at the end of 1940, the eight-year correspondence would make Tinkham one of Pound's "recruits" and attempt to engage him in an ongoing discourse not only with Pound himself, but also with those with whom he encouraged a more productive acquaintance.

Thus Pound tries to reinforce and refine what Daniel Pearlman calls Tinkham's "Social Credit leanings" (422) by consistently affirming the ideas of Major Douglas, whose name crops up periodically in the letters from 1935 through 1939; by encouraging him to seek out or inquire into other politicians and intellectuals, such as Senator Lynn Frazier of North Dakota and the journalist Amos Pinchot (Letter 35), whose ideas were compatible with Social Credit theory; by suggesting that he adopt a nurturing posture toward certain promising Congressional novices, such as the "bright INFANT" Jerry Voorhis of California, whose ideas were on the right track but still malleable ("don't shoot the kid until you have looked at his teeth" [Letter 44]); and by subjecting Social Credit itself to critical examination, a critique that comes into sharpest focus in the context of the failure of the Alberta experiment (Letter 43).

In addition to encouraging Tinkham's commitment to Social Credit, Pound attempts to stimulate his thinking about economics in general and the political implications of a decent economic system by bombarding him with compatible fragments from a mixed bag of thinkers and doers other than Douglas himself. The letters are full of references to economists like Montgomery Butchart (Letters 16 and 24) and Christopher Hollis (Letters 15, 16, 20, and 44); journalists like Robert McNair Wilson (Letters 12, 46, and 87) and Francis Delaisi (Letters 18 and 28); public officials like Edmondo Rossoni (Letters 15, 16, 18, and 43) and Walther Funk (Letter 99); philosophers like Confucius (Letters 53 and 57) and Scotus Erigina (Letter 81); and even, when they happen to advocate a Poundian notion, bankers like Rupert Beckett (Letter 15) and Reginald McKenna (Letters 15 and 20). While these and similar references are usually elliptical and suggestive rather than discursive, they nonetheless create a pattern of reference that is both repetitive and cumulative, reinforcing and expanding (much like *The Cantos* themselves), thereby enfolding Tinkham into the fabric of the discourse and encouraging him to join it. Pound does not always tell him what to think and do, but he does show him where he believes the clearest thinking and the most effective action are taking place. The effect is to situate Tinkham within an international network that is intellectually "charged," to place him in a context where certain core ideas can generate a new economic system in the catalytic presence of intellectual interaction and reciprocal influence. In other words, it is to place him within Pound's own Rapallo vortex.

All claims of "vortex Rapallo" notwithstanding, Pound wished to engage Tinkham in the practical affairs of the United States, and to this end the "discourse" should take place on American soil. Therefore a second category of references and encouragements, which centers on Washington but radiates to other centers of political activity, includes other Congressmen and Senators, such as William Borah of Idaho (Letters 16 and

72), Joseph Martin of Massachusetts (Letters 78 and 81), Henry Stiles Bridges of New Hampshire (Letter 38), and Burton K. Wheeler of Montana (Letter 38), as well as Republican bosses like J. D. M. Hamilton (Letters 29 and 30) and Samuel Pryor (Letters 81, 84, and 100). These are the people Pound wanted Tinkham to work with in a coordinated effort to remove Roosevelt from the White House.

While the letters clearly demonstrate that Pound took the greater initiative in network-formation, whether for political action or economic edification, Tinkham himself tried to reciprocate when Pound came to the United States in 1939 in his quixotic effort to forestall American entry into the Second World War. In his letter of 15 May 1939, Tinkham encloses letters of introduction for Pound to a number of influential people in Massachusetts, including politicians and newspaper editors (see Letter 72, n1) whom Pound might have found useful. While these letters did not catch up with Pound in time for him to use them (see Letter 74), Tinkham's offer of assistance was clearly more than a mere political gesture. He really did want to put Pound in touch with the Massachusetts power base. Since his home state was the one place where his own influence was strongest, he probably felt he could help Pound the most in Massachusetts. Moreover, he himself wanted to know Pound's assessment of the thinking in Boston. "I was much interested," he writes in Letter 74, "in your comments concerning your interview with Mr. Herter." On the other hand, Tinkham's introductions show that he took Pound and his ideas seriously, referring to him as an "economist" in addition to "the distinguished poet." If he had had any serious doubts about Pound's economic ideas, he probably would not have recommended him in this manner to people on whose political support he depended, nor is it likely that he would have subjected these men to so outspoken a man as Pound if he did not think that they could benefit from his ideas. In sum, Tinkham must have regarded his effort to introduce Pound to his Massachusetts contacts as beneficial to all concerned. It was an effort that was well within the spirit of Pound's own civilization-building agenda.

That Pound was successful in recruiting Tinkham into his "civilization" is clear by the content and tone of the letters themselves, not to mention the degree to which Tinkham faithfully upheld his end of the correspondence. In the first place, the exchange of ideas and opinions expressed in the letters mark out a common ground. On the fundamental issues of economics and foreign policy, Pound and Tinkham were in general agreement. Pound's preoccupation with economics, particularly the need to think clearly about the nature of money, is matched by Tinkham's careful analysis of the economic situation, which he articulates most extensively in his letter of 31 March 1937 (Letter 39), concluding on a characteristically pessimistic and partisan note:

> These three elements, basic commodity prices, taxes and labor costs, determine the cost of living, so the cost of living must rise, and this irresistibly, causing a fall in the purchasing power of national and international currencies. I say "international" currencies as well as national currencies because all the larger countries are pursuing about the same course.
>
> From all this, as you can well see, will come political and social chaos. The denouement in the United States will come very probably between 1938 and 1941. I should rather be held to this span of years in this prediction, although quite tentatively I am picking 1939 as the year.

On the other hand Pound's perceptions of the international conspiracy of bankers and munitions makers, and the intertwining interests of government, financiers, and the press, parallel Tinkham's fears and convictions about foreign entanglements, whether they be manifest in foundations like the Carnegie Endowment (*Cong. Rec.* 3 Feb. 1933: 3336-39), the communist conspiracy (*Cong. Rec.* 14 May 1935: 7526-34), or Roosevelt's desire to involve the United States in a European war:

> If there is war, as it is the only political "out" for Roosevelt, he will do everything to get us in. I predicted a course of events with that ending to our Chief of Staff in April or May 1936. (Letter 76)

This common ground, moreover, extends to their opinions of two key personalities, Mussolini and Roosevelt himself. Of the former, Tinkham has this to say: "Mussolini certainly has had a great triumph and in his age and generation is a great man" (Letter 17). And of the latter:

> There is plenty to hear [about America's relation to the European war in 1940], and a great deal of froth and foolishness, framed in by the greatest uncertainty in every direction with a psychopathic hysteric presiding over all. (Letter 85)

While this "common ground" was clearly important to the correspondence since it gave the two men something to talk about without serious disagreement, an even more important factor was Tinkham's quality of mind, both in fact and in terms of Pound's perceptions. As Tinkham demonstrates in these letters, he was an independent thinker and an articulate explainer; moreover, at least from Pound's standpoint, he was both lucid and open-minded. These intellectual qualities, combined with the fact that he took Pound seriously and proved to be a good listener, constituted an audience for Pound that all but guaranteed a sustained correspondence. On one hand, Tinkham's intellectual qualities, apart from engaging Pound's admiration, provided an effective sounding board, a mind in the presence of which Pound could refine his own articulations. On the other hand, Tinkham's receptive attitude encouraged the profusion of those articulations. Taken together, these qualities supported the pedagogical strain in Pound's rhetorical stance, a strain that was both central and dominant since education, or the dissemination of information, was fundamental to *what* Pound wanted to achieve (a revitalized civilization) and *how* he aimed to achieve it (political action).

As the letters demonstrate, Pound was pedagogically successful, but a proper understanding of this success requires further explanation and qualification of the notion of Pound's pedagogy and its relationship to Tinkham. To begin with, it is necessary to emphasize the limits of his pedagogical aim: as pedagogue, Pound's aim was to convey to Tinkham information about economics, politics, and related national and world affairs, and to do it in such a way that the information would effectively register on Tinkham's intelligence. Given this aim Pound's attitude toward Tinkham is not the usual attitude of a teacher toward a student; rather, it is the attitude of a teacher toward someone else who is neither a student nor a colleague, someone with whom he has no hierarchical relation whatsoever but who nevertheless shows interest in the information conveyed. It is a relationship that allows the "teacher" to teach but does not require a "student" who learns.

Tinkham, in other words, does not move from a state of ignorance to a state of knowledge; he merely, and for the most part silently, assimilates new information into the sophisticated body of knowledge that he already has, and occasionally, when Pound asks for it, contributes information of his own, as he does in Letters 13 and 39. This information is sometimes "corrected" by the pedagogue (see, for example, Letter 14, in which Pound dissociates the notions of "convertibility" and "supply"), but even the "correction" is more accurately absorbed into, rather than taken as a replacement for, old knowledge. Whatever Tinkham might choose to do with the information was outside the scope of the pedagogical aim. (To provoke action on Tinkham's part is a different rhetorical aim, one that will be addressed below.)

Another aspect of Pound's pedagogy is that the structure of his "teaching" alternates between a straightforward, consistently focused, albeit elliptical analysis of a subject to a more fragmented and discontinuous approach that is similar to the ideogrammic method he uses in *The Cantos*. An example of the more conventional structure is Letter 28. In this letter, written in October 1936, he addresses a question Tinkham had asked him during his recent visit with Pound at Venice (which was the only time the two men actually met): "Will the price of gold go up?" After answering emphatically "YES," he piles two plus pages of qualifications, dissociations, and implications on top of his initial "generic" response, thus adding texture to his argument in true academic fashion, or in a fashion that would be perceived as academic were it not for the ellipses in the otherwise continuous argument, ellipses that are magnified by the erratic typography.

In contrast to the direct, conventional structure, Letter 38, dated 27 February 1937, represents Pound's more associative, ideogrammic thinking at work (or at "play," to inject a Barthesian impression that may be more to the point). This type of thinking, as it pertains to Pound's poetry, is "ideogrammic" because it centers on the notion of the "ideogram," which is an idea presented through juxtaposition of concrete particulars, usually without connective words or phrases (Gefin xvi). In Letter 38 Pound adopts this poetic strategy to communicate a complex image of politics. The "concrete particulars," or components, that comprise the letter are as follows:

> Component 1 – the press: "cuttings" from the Washington "Pust"; "truth" is questioned.
> Component 2 – presidents/presidential hopefuls: Harding, Vandenberg, Bridges, and Dewey; level of understanding and receptivity questioned.
> Component 3 – parental duty: Dewey et. al. as children; Tinkham as parent; right thinking is a matter of intellectual maturity.
> Component 4 – the Dutchmen: Congressman Joseph Martin vis-à-vis Martin Van Buren; Van Buren as standard for "economic comprehension," the "BUT" against which present politicians are measured.
> Component 5 – presidential hopefuls, again: Bridges and Wheeler; "economic comprehension" is questioned.
> Component 6 – the press, again: support for Republican candidate (Vandenberg, Dewey) equals guaranteed Democratic victory; the smell of conspiracy, the odor of dissembling.
> Component 7 – the "son-in-law racket": Alexander Hamilton and Philip Schuyler, with echoes of the Anthony Eden-Gervase

Beckett connection (Letters 12 and 14); conspiracy of international finance; perversion of parental duty component : the "snots...play for 'YOUTH', which they think they can bamboozle." Component 8 – historical reference: "notes on J/Adams and the Chinese Emperors"; suggestive juxtaposition; anticipates Chinese and Adams ideograms in *The Cantos*.

When perceived in their composite, these particulars form an ideogram – call it the ideogram of presidential politics – that conveys some of the uncertainties of such politics, especially as they undermine one's confidence in candidates whose nascent economic ideas are taking shape in an atmosphere of conspiracy and manipulation.

Finally, it should be borne in mind that Pound's pedagogy is pedagogy, not propaganda. The difference between the educator and the propagandist is that the former engages his audience within a discourse that is free of controversy (Lasswell 3). That Pound addresses Tinkham in this context is clear enough, the "common ground" discussed above is sufficient evidence to dispel any notion of controversy. More than mere agreement, however, the letters show that Pound thought of Tinkham, just as he thought of himself, as a mentor for his intellectually "younger" colleagues, as a kind of teacher in his own right. In other words, he saw Tinkham as an elite or privileged audience, one that was, in Chaim Perelman's phrase, "distinct from the common run of men" (34). Moreover, he saw him as one with whom he could share not only ideas and opinions, but also the more intimate attitudes conveyed through linguistic nuance. Pound's seeming penchant for homespun speech, insofar as it emphasizes by exaggeration the "ordinary" in his unique linguistic mix, signifies his comfort and strong sense of communion with his audience. In addition, it supports his pedagogical aim by promoting agreement. As Perelman points out,

> The relationship between ordinary language and admitted ideas is not fortuitous: ordinary language is by itself the manifestation of agreement, of community of thought, by the same right as the received ideas. Ordinary language can help to promote agreement on the ideas. (153)

What is perhaps more telling, Pound's frequent "lapses" of diction and particularly his gross alterations of the surnames of Roosevelt and his circle shore up, through implied complicity, the privileged status of the discourse. On this point Perelman is again instructive:

> . . . mutilation of a proper name or distortion of a text usually attest to a certain contempt for the person or thing referred to. These negligences can create a complicity with the hearer .... Use

of a deliberately poor or clumsy vocabulary may serve the same purpose. (164)

Because Pound perceives Tinkham as already part of an elite audience, he does not have to convert him to a different system of ideas, values, and attitudes; therefore, the propagandist in Pound, if it exists at all, remains latent in his correspondence with Tinkham since there is no motive to release it.

If one of Pound's rhetorical motives in these letters is pedagogical, another is a call to action; and depending on the nature of the action called for, Tinkham was more or less responsive. If the action was merely to supply information, Tinkham was quite accommodating, even if it meant spending his own or his staff's time to do the necessary research or locate the relevant documents. See, for example, Tinkham's letter of 25 June 1937 (Letter 47), in which he encloses information on the Empire Credit Foundation and a copy of the Patman Bill in response to Pound's requests, or his secretary's letter of 11 May 1940 (Letter 93), in which she encloses the Treasury Department information that Pound wanted. On the other hand, if the action involved any kind of commitment on Tinkham's part, such as introducing a bill in Congress or entering the presidential race, the response was not forthcoming. Thus Tinkham served Pound well in his bureaucratic capacity of provider of information, but he was consistently unresponsive to requests that called for the exercise of whatever power and influence he might have had. That is, he did nothing to put Pound's ideas into effect. As a pedagogue Pound was successful in getting his message across, but as a motivater he failed to inspire practical action.

The most curious aspect of this rhetorical failure is that Pound persevered in his role of advisor, exhorter, and political strategist despite the lack of any indication that his advice, exhortations, and strategies would be acted upon. Indeed, judging from Tinkham's return letters most of Pound's overtures in this regard were tacitly rejected, while others, such as his proposition that Tinkham run for president, were politely acknowledged as mere flattery. Indeed, in Tinkham's letter of 20 June 1936 (Letter 17), he makes a glancing, and characteristically formal, reference to "your very flattering communication of March 11" and then moves on to matters of presumably greater import, notably his upcoming European vacation. To attempt to explain this seemingly futile perseverance of Pound's requires shifting focus from the rhetorical to the psychological dimension of the correspondence.

At the risk of suggesting technical, psychological connotations that are beyond the realm of my expertise, I can think of no better word than "delusion" to help explain the curiosity of Pound's dogged pursuit of rhetorical goals that, from an objective standpoint, seem futile. To appreciate the point, consider Pound's assumed role of political strategist that dominates many of the letters.

As Daniel Pearlman suggests in his article on the Pound-to-Borah letters, Pound, as early as May 1934, envisioned himself as "the unofficial Brains Trust of the next president of the United States" (421). Pearlman's comment refers to Pound's self-assigned role as economic and political advisor to Idaho's Senator William Borah, who sought the presidency in 1936. As Pearlman further points out, after the Republican defeat in the 1936 elections Pound pinned his hopes for 1940 on George H. Tinkham (422), hopes that the Tinkham correspondence itself clearly documents. It is worth mentioning at this point that his alliance with these two presidential "hopefuls"–the first a candidate in fact, the second a candidate only in Pound's imagination–reveals two aspects of Pound's character that help to explain his personal campaign against Roosevelt: for one thing, he was *serious* about defeating Roosevelt at the polls; for another, he really *believed* that he himself could be instrumental in that venture.

The basis for Pound's support of Borah and Tinkham, apart from economic philosophy, was his belief that Roosevelt could be defeated and his judgment that the Republican party itself had been and still was partially responsible for Roosevelt's success. In a letter to Tinkham dated 4 November 1936 (Letter 29), Pound calls the GOP a "dictatorship from the DuPonts and Wall St .... with a nonentity [Alfred M. Landon] at the head of the ticket," refers to its policies as "sheer intellectual cowardice," and accuses it of mounting "a purely negative and cowardly opposition to Roosevelt that has been a WASH OUT."

While it is clear that he thought the Republicans needed new, courageous, and articulate leadership, it is equally clear that he had his own ideas about the direction in which that leadership should move. Expatriate though he was, Pound seems to have had a greater sensitivity to the national mandate than did the Republican bosses back home, for he perceived that the right direction was implicit in the New Deal itself. He wrote Tinkham again the next day (5 November 1936, Letter 30) to advise that the "old skeleton" of the GOP should take up "some clear and decent issue. a way out: that is to say an ISSUE

FROM the Nude eel. NO question of changing just a FEW votes in 1940." Then he continues:

> You are not going to oust Frankfurter with mere non-intellectual tosh; and a few soft boiled lies that millions of people now KNOW to be hoakum ....
>
> Only way to beat Nude Eel ideology is to get a BETTER one, something with a drive/ not merely old fat.

And he reiterates the theme in a letter of 23 November 1936 (Letter 31):

> My belief that F. D. R. will grab ALL the good issues/ and the only effective opposition will be to get the BEST ones BEFORE he does. and then HOLD 'em.

As these excerpts from his letters to Tinkham suggest, Pound's assessment of the political situation seems not to have been unreasonable. However, if you consider his perception of his own role in rectifying that situation, you come away with an altogether different impression. The self-importance that is implicit in the advisory role that Pound had assumed with Borah carried over into his correspondence with Tinkham. In a letter of 6 February 1936 (Letter 15) he writes:

> When I say a serious [economic] enquiry I mean one where people like Odon Por, C. H. Douglas and myself wd. get a chance to cross examine the Tugwells, Warburgs, Spragues, Warrens, etc.

That Pound regarded himself as an authority on economics is clear enough; the prospect of Pound cross-examining members of and advisors to the Roosevelt administration, presumably within the chambers of the Capitol itself, seems to have no basis in reality. Moreover, the delusory quality of his scenario is underscored by fact: when he actually tried to intervene during his Washington visit of 1939, he was either rebuffed or ignored, his conversation with Agriculture Secretary Wallace notwithstanding (Stock, *Life* 361-62).

One month later, in a letter dated 11 March 1936 (Letter 16), Pound speaks of his own role in the "prospective" presidential campaign:

> On my part it means working on private letters to you rather than in splashing ideas over printed pages.
>
> I don't mean I wd. quit publishing economic articles, but there wd/ have to be coordination, and the mere pleasure of uttering ideas, wd. have to be fitted into the probable effect of printing them.

The modest, businesslike tone of this description of his role might suggest anything but self-importance, but when you consider that the whole notion of the Tinkham campaign was pure Poundian fantasy, and that, judging from the return letters, Tinkham himself had no intention of running for the presidency, the modesty is strikingly peculiar because the proposition itself is fantastic.

The culmination of the thread of delusion that runs through Pound's letters to Tinkham comes in a letter of January 1937 (Letter 36):

> [Lecture agent William Colston] Leigh offering me tour in the U. S. CD/ it be any USE?? I suppose I shd. read poesy and 'lecture' on littercheer...IF etc// matter of timing whether it cd. [be] used as feeler or to get things into the air .... At any rate my transport and expenses wd. be covered ....
>
> BUT I shd/ want guidance before hand as to what was possible and/or advisable. ALSO the choice of time very important. He suggests winter of 37 or Fall of '38.
>
> Neither time any use to ME ....
>
> And other more interesting ways of using my TIME...
>
> there wd. have to be a REASON for a tour, more than being looked at.

The "REASON," of course, would be to reconnoiter, to test the political waters in the American hinterland, to spread the WORD of a Tinkham presidency. It would be to enact the role that Pound had conceived for himself; more to the point, it would be to enact the role that he *alone* conceived, and that he conceived out of whole cloth. But if his conception had even less grounding in the real world than did the Tinkham presidency itself, where did it come from?

The answer, I think, lies in Pound's poetry, or it lies in his poetic imagination. The notion of the poet (or the poet's minstrel) as advance man or political operative had captured Pound's imagination some thirty years earlier when he was studying the Provençal troubadours. Indeed, a poet such as Bertran de Born, whose poetry often mixed the sentiments of love with the politics of war, might well have been the prototype for his own persona of 1937. Peter Makin, in his book *Provence and Pound*, makes the following comment on de Born's poetry:

> One might guess that the love half [of de Born's poetry] served to gain entry to the courts of Poitou and Limousin, ruled by their "salon-queens," from which the propaganda of the war half might effectively spread. If a *joglar* [de Born's minstrel] gained entrance or attention more easily by announcing that he had a song about the lady of the house, the troubadour could very well insert a mention of her, just so as to have his man welcomed at that particular castle. And so, if we look on the map and find that the traceable ladies in a particular song form a neat circle around the

troubadour's potential enemy, as...they do in *Dompna puois*, may
we not suspect some kind of political intrigue? (27-28)

This is precisely the kind of intrigue that Pound develops in his
own version of de Born's *Dompna puois*. In "Near Perigord" the
covert function of the minstrel is to venture into the centers of
power where his master's political interests might best be served,
and there to become that master's eyes and ears and tongue.

If this "persona" of the poet as political operative
had lain dormant in Pound's imagination over the years, the exi-
gencies of 1936 might well have awakened it; and given his incli-
nation to convert thought to action, the awakened persona
would have been the perfect vehicle. Under the pretense of
giving lectures or reading poetry, Pound would play minstrel to
Tinkham's de Born, or he would assume the dual role of poet
and *joglar*, bringing his own eyes, ears, and voice into the coun-
tryside, all in a *political* effort to unseat, not the Count at Perigord, but the President in the White House. However, since the
real world, especially America of the 1930s, would not support
the conception, the persona merely enriched the delusion.

Deluded or not, Pound was undaunted. Throughout
the correspondence he persevered as advisor and/or strategist,
convinced of the rightness of his perceptions and the feasibility
of his propositions. Even in the later stages of the correspondence, when Tinkham's disinclination to follow up on Pound's
calls for action had long since become a pattern that would have
discouraged another person, Pound continued to hammer away,
albeit with increasing frustration. In a letter of 20 January 1939
(Letter 68), which was the *second* letter to Tinkham on that day,
he lashes out at Tinkham himself, as if yet another, more force-
ful appeal could break the Congressman's inertia.

> sorry to be so frequent, but paragraph in Eclaireur de Nice sets
> me off. It says Roosevelt wants you to PROLONG his financial
> powers. DAMN it do you never READ the constitution. Of course
> Baruch and co/ don't give a damn about that document. ARE you
> still on the committee for affairs concerning the Pres? Congress
> has power to issue money etc/ ... You are merely illegal if you
> hand over right to issue money to, let us say, the Chief J. Justice.
>
> Frankie NEVER legally had these powers. Why go on com-
> pounding a felony or whatever.

Whether or not Pound was deluded as to the significance of his self-appointed role in the deliverance of America,
his stubborn adherence to that role can be explained by his need
to stay afloat in a world that of itself would not sustain him. It
was his veil of Leucothea, without which he could have no hope.
More importantly, his belief in his ability to influence public

affairs was central to the Rapallo vortex. He had to keep that vortex churning; if the center did not hold, the whole thing would fall apart. Seen in this light, the Ezra Pound of the Tinkham correspondence projects a suggestive image of the public Pound whose wartime activities led to his personal tragedy. Psychologically dependent on the perpetuation of his vortex, he was prisoner to necessity, but it was a prison whose walls were pure motion, an equilibrium of centripetal and centrifugal forces that were imperceptible to the outside world. The world, rejecting the vortex and blind to the prison, recognized only the prisoner. Ironically, and tragically for Pound, it took him for a prisoner of its own.

When Tinkham, who was something of a big game hunter, had arrived in Rome on a European tour in 1936, he sent Pound a "letter of greeting" (Letter 19). In his return letter (Letter 20), Pound included a comment that, in retrospect, is poignantly ironic:

> No big game here for you to shoot, only one unfortunate lion, but you might shoot the responsible people for putting the animal in a cage that is MUCH too small.

1.   Pound to Tinkham

6 Feb XI[1] [1933]

Representative G.H. Tinkham
Washington

Sir
     AND CHEERS !! Damn well time someone said so. Peace
O.K. and all very nice but that gas bag Nic. Butler has
so far as I can make out done nothing but {GGGGGGGGGG}
sabotage the study of the CAUSES of war ever since he
got his racket.[2]
                    Count Mensdorff wrote to Nic. But. back
about 1927 (I can look up precise date if any use)
telling him that there ARE economic causes of war, that
at least some of the causes of wars are more or less
known and that the g.d. foundation was hired to study 'em.[3]
     These foundations are a tax on public (ten millions
cost half a million a year).   IF the foundation
does something of more use to pubk. than pubk. cd. or wd.
do for self.   All jake.   But a gang of profs. merely
sponging on a corpse .... seems as if the house ought to
be pincher, malversation of funds.
                    Guggenheim foundation incompetent.   Aydelotte and
co.[4] about as competent to pick writers as I wd. be
to judge Kentucky horses.   But the Carnegie undoubtedly
the worst scandal.
                    You dont make peace by messing up internal
order of any country.   Till man can feel himself part
*** [page(s) missing[5]]

1. The Roman numeral XI refers to year eleven of the Fascist era. During this
period Pound often dated his letters in this fashion.
2. Pound refers to a speech Tinkham made in the House of Representatives on 3
February 1933. In his speech Tinkham attacked the Carnegie Endowment and its
president, Nicholas Murray Butler. Tinkham claimed that the Carnegie
Endowment and similar organizations were "disloyal and seditious" and sought
to "destroy the independence of the United States, to subvert her national
integrity, and to involve her in advance in the next European war." Tinkham
based this last claim on what he saw as the primary goal of the Endowment: the
entry of the United States into the League of Nations (*Cong. Rec.* 3 Feb. 1933:
3336-39). The contention that the foundation should investigate the causes of
war was Pound's, not Tinkham's, and was not voiced in the speech. Tinkham

enclosed a copy of his speech in his letter to Pound on 28 February 1933 (see Letter 2).

3. Count Albert von Mensdorff-Pouilly-Dietrichstein (1861-1945) was the Austro-Hungarian ambassador to Great Britain (1904-14), delegate to the League of Nations, and European agent for the Carnegie Endowment ("Mensdorff"). Stock reports that Mensdorff's letter to the Endowment, dated 18 June 1928, was actually written jointly with Pound, but signed only by Mensdorff. In the letter Mensdorff-Pound lists the "causes" as follows:

"1. Intense production and sale of munitions....

"2. Overproduction and dumping, leading to trade rivalries and irritation.

"3. The intrigues of interested cliques" (276).

Elsewhere, Pound lists these same three items, in paraphrase, as the *known* causes of war" ("Peace," *Selected Prose* 222).

4. Frank Aydelotte (1880-1956), then president of Swarthmore College, was advisor to Simon Guggenheim in planning the John Simon Guggenheim Memorial Foundation for the support of science and the arts (Davis, John 256-57).

5. The missing passage probably contains some of Pound's Confucian philosophy about the importance of order in all levels of society, beginning with individual and domestic order.

2.   Tinkham to Pound

February 28, 1933

E. Pound, Esquire
Rapallo
Genova, Italy

My dear Mr. Pound:
  Sincere thanks for your kind communication
of February 6. I take pleasure in sending to you
herewith a printed copy of my speech of February 3 in
the House of Representatives.[1]

  With all good wishes, I am
        Sincerely yours,
  [signed] GEORGE HOLDEN TINKHAM

Encl.

1. See Letter 1, n2.

3.   Pound to Tinkham

[after 28 February 1933]

Hon. G.H. Tinkham
Washington D.C.

My dear Mr Tinkham
Thanks very much. I am glad to see full
text of yr. (Feb. 3) speech.
Wouldn't it be possible to "get" Butler
and co., not on basis of Carnegie's general letch for
the old country, but on the terms of Carnegie's letter
endowing the "Foundation".[1]
They have certainly violated the "trust"
I mean they have assiduously kept OFF all investigation
of causes of war.
AND they either know it, or ought to
know it. I mean they have been informed, and their only
reason for not knowing is that they have a secretary to
file documents and NOT to read 'em to the trustees.

Mr Bunting, who has studied their last report more carefully
than I have, suggests that their research is mainly
an enquiry as to how to make the next war more
efficient.[2]

Considering the extent to which ENDOWMENTS, if not
all and sundry, at least a great number, have been
used to stultify intellectual life in America, your

*** [bottom of page missing]

after it finishes with the ineffable Nic. B.
I hope your resolution was carried.[3]

It's pretty good betting that the Carnegie will not diffuse
the information contained in "Mercanti di Cannoni"
   reprint from La Stampa di Torino.

large Parisian
Best inf. I can get, there are four {french} papers
not owned by La Comite des Forges[4] (plus two extreme
            Populaire
left; {HHHHHHHH} and L Humanite)

Petit Parisien, Petit Journal, Journal and L Oeuvre.

When you find any uncoloured news in London Press
you might send me a cable.

sincerely yours

1. Tinkham offered evidence in his speech of 3 February 1933 that Andrew Carnegie yearned for the reunification of Great Britain and the United States (*Cong. Rec.* 3 Feb. 1933: 3337-38). Carnegie's letter, reprinted in the *New York Times* on 15 December 1910, makes no explicit reference to investigating the causes of war, although such an investigation was within the spirit of the letter. However, Trustee James Brown Scott, who was State Department solicitor at the time, did recommend that an investigation into the causes of war should be first on the Endowment's agenda ("$10,000,000" 1-2). Cf. Letter 1, n2.

2. Basil Bunting (1900-1985), the British poet, visted Pound at Rapallo and lived there from time to time. A conscientious objector, he had spent six months in jail following World War I (Terrell, vol. 2 371).

3. Tinkham's resolution, which he submitted upon delivery of his speech of 3 February 1933, was "to investigate the political activities of all organizations, foundations, endowments, and associations which have attempted or are attempting to influence political opinion and political action by any means whatsoever, with reference to the foreign policy of the United States" (*Cong. Rec.* 3 Feb. 1933: 3339). The resolution was not "carried." For Tinkham's contemplated submission of a similar resolution, see Letter 5.

4. *La Comité des Forges* was a powerful French trust representing the steel industry. It was influential in French politics and policy, especially regarding foreign affairs, and was linked to war profiteering (Seldes 118-19).

4.   Pound to Tinkham

9 March
1935 March
    1935
The Hon. G.H. Tinkham
Sir
  The Hon. G.H. Tinck
        I am very glad to read (Santa Fe New Mexican[1]) that you
mean to show up the Carnegie Endowment (the Rockefeller, I know
less about but wd/be glad of details.) More power to yr/
elbow.
        Butler deserves no pity. Those buzzards have spent half a
million a year taxed out of the people, and they have steadily
avoided exposing or investigating the economic causes of war.
            All these big endowments feed a bureaucracy, and
what they do toward the "purpose" avowed or "intended" by their
founders" is not always clear.
            As I am doing a weekly column on American affairs[2]
which does percolate back into American offices, I shd/be glad
to have congressional record for days when you get going.
            I take it the Peace endowment is what the notice
refers to. The library endowment is probably slack, and
led by the nose by N.Y. editors who wd/be better dead.
        Yale Review with its centenarian edtr/and Salter (my
sufferin' catfish is there no English corpse so dead that some
American flunky won't trot out and caress it) as star
"economist", liar, staller etc... might also be dynamited.[3]
                obt. sv.

1. On 26 March 1935 Pound published the first of a "sporadic" series of columns
in the Santa Fe *New Mexican* entitled "Ez Sez: Being Some Pithy Promulgations"
(Clark 420).
2. The "weekly column" was probably "American Notes" in *The New English
Weekly*.
3. Sir James Arthur Salter (1881-1975), director of the economic and finance
section of the League of Nations and advocate of the 1933 World Economic
Conference and the U.S. Federal Reserve System, was a British economist who,
during the 1930s, contributed pieces on economics to *The Yale Review* (Rickett).
The "centenarian edtr" of *The Yale Review* was Wilbur L. Cross. Cross, who was
then 73 years old, had been editor since 1911 and would continue in that role
until 1940. He was also governor of Connecticut (1931-39) ("Cross").

5.   Tinkham to Pound

April 2, 1935

E. Pound, Esquire
via Marsala 12-5
Rapallo
Genova, Italy

My dear Mr. Pound:

Sincere thanks for your communication of
March 9. I regret that it has not been possible for
me to reply to it sooner but recently I have been
quite overwhelmed with work of an urgent character.
Enclosed is a copy of a speech which I made
on the Carnegie Endowment about two years ago.[1] I
shall probably move at the proper time for an investigation of the expenditures of this and other foundations for propaganda purposes, and in the event that
I have any speech on the subject printed, a copy will
be sent to you.
With kindest regards and with all good
wishes, I remain

Sincerely yours,
[signed] GEORGE HOLDEN TINKHAM

1. This is the 3 February 1933 speech that Tinkham had already sent to Pound on
28 February 1933 (see Letter 2).

6.   Pound to Tinkham

[May 1935]

The Hon.
George Holden Tinkham
Washington

Dear Mr Tinkham

The arrest of Jacques Roumain in Haiti
needs investigation. It is an outrage that a writer
of Roumain's standing and sensibility should be treated as a
common bum.[1]
It is the kind of foolishness that makes
all the young intelligentsia see red and hate [the] very
form of order.

Thanks for yr/letter re Butler. The WHOLE of education
needs overhauling. 80% of all professorships that teach
anything
bearing on life seem to be given to men who do nothing but
IMPEDE research. Heaven knows there is room for thought
and a need for correlation of KNOWLEDGE in economics.
We wont get it by the London so called School, or the
american professorial snob who takes on english opinion
(and especially error) 20 years late. Novelty as novelty
may be a diversion for dilletantes, but a stale novelty,
a lie 20 years old has, as far as I can see, very
few merits.

1. Jacques Roumain, then considered the foremost poet and writer in Haiti, had
been imprisoned on fabricated charges of treason. He was an outspoken critic of
the Haitian government under dictator Stensio Vincent (Bradley).

7.   Tinkham to Pound

August 20, 1935

Professor Ezra Pound

c/o Messrs. Stanley Nott, Limited
69 Grafton Street
Fitzroy Square
London, W.1, England

My dear Professor Pound:

Sincere thanks for your communication
from Salzburg and also for the complimentary
copy of your book, "Jefferson and/or Mussolini",
which was received several days ago from the
publishers, Messrs. Stanley Nott, Limited.
I shall read this publication with much interest,
and I appreciate your kind thought in having it sent
to me.

With cordial regards, I remain
Sincerely yours,
[signed] GEORGE HOLDEN TINKHAM

8. Pound to Tinkham

                    310 San Gregorio
                                    Venice   2. Sept. [1935]

Hon. G.H. Tinkham
Washington

Dear Mr Tinkham

    Whether ANYone in the U.S. wd. have
or has had the patience to wade through the tempest
of English, French and Italian papers due to Abyssinia AND
ALBERTA, social credit landslide, I don't know.[1] I find it
hard work to read ONE American newspaper two weeks
later.
    If the following summary of Financial News, Morn. Post,
different french papers, Temps, Matin, etc.
and the Italian press is any use to you, go on and
wade thru it.
    If it is all old stuff by the time this
reaches you, don't bother.

Schacht due in London.   Monty Norman in Canada, gone too
                                    both of 'em
late to stop or blackmail Alberta, jews and friends,[2]

    Tannery is SAME position as Louis XVI,
foreign aid in struggle against french people.
    Bank of Eng. a private company, but that ASS
Morgenthau is officially the U.S.A.
    and Tannery SAYING he had got AID to
help in POLITICAL crisis.
    Rotten as the french press is (vide Rafallovich
papers) some frog must in time observe this analogy.[3]
England allied to the enemies of the people in both
france and germany CANT be in very sound position.

Stephen Lausanne[4] reprints VERY CLEAR text of Suez Canal
contract.
    British Tory press, quoting the rootenest
french left (the soppy, worse than Manchester drivveler
L. Bloom[5] etc.) to back up British imperialism.
    ///
As to economic reform

You can save property rights IF you dissociate
property from CAPITAL, which is DIFFERENT.   Capital
is a lein on others, property is NOT.

Usury differs from the increment of association.

As long economics profs. in Harvard and 40 other
universities teach drivvle which DOES NOT dissociate

different economic factors, the whole teaching of econ.
remains pseudoscience of the most dangerous sort,
                         ANY attempt at order gets branded
bolshevik etc.
                    After ten years "lid", british press now
RATTLED by Alberta. Telegraph calling Aberhart[6]
a "socialist organization"
                              when British socialists are
the LAST people who will stand for C.H. Douglas.[7]
                  and {M. post} Financial News talking about
currency cranks who CLAIM there is a shortage
of purchasing power.
                                   *** and at that
point (with millions on DOLE. idiotically, but presumably
because some lack of purchasing power had been noticed
somewhere or other.

I wish somebody with a grain of sense wd. see Douglas
on his way to Alberta, or failing that talk with
young Larkin (Crate Larkin) v.p. Larkin Co.
          680 Seneca St. Buffalo.[8]

N. Angell must be merely gaga.   but typical pacifist
prefers pan-european war to having a little one in
Abyssinia.[9] Gen Page Croft rather good in yester/Morn. Post.[10]
Zaharoff said to have disappeared again.[11]
No doubt Russian element wants pan/europ war, in hope
of general revolutionary shindy.
Trouble with Brain Trust is HALF-ignorance. I ONCE
read a book by a Prof. named Dexter Kimball, containing some
good sense.[12] Haven't heard of his being mixed in
shall we frivolously say the Frankfurter/sausage.[13]

At any rate if they wd. start their damned economics
by using ONE WORD to mean ONE thing (and not six or

seven different things), and thereafter refrain from false dilemma, such as "Mr. R. MUST go either to Pittsburg or Brooklyn") we might hope for a few simple steps toward a saner order.

My Jeff/Muss writ. over two years ago. I hear the method of slapping down the incongruous and uncooked facts, and leaving the reader to THINK, is annoying a number of people. especially the British.

[no closing]

1. The threat of war between Italy and Abyssinia (Ethiopia) was acute in September 1935. Italy attacked in October. In Alberta, Canada, a social credit government had been elected on 22 August 1935, with William Aberhart as premier ("Alberta is Swept").

2. The former Reichsbank president (1923-30), Hjalmar Horace Greeley Schacht (1877-1970) was German Minister of Economics (1934-37) ("Schacht"). The British press had reported that he was bound for London to obtain a loan through the Bank of England. The Reichsbank denied the story, citing Montagu Norman's absence from England as sufficient evidence to belie the claim ("Montagu Norman Arrives"). Norman (1871-1950), then governor of the Bank of England (1920-44) ("Norman"), had arrived in Canada on 11 August and would embark on his return trip on 6 September ("Montagu Norman Sails").

3. Jean Tannery (1878-1939), then governor of the Bank of France (1935-36) ("Tannery"), had received U.S. aid in France's franc crisis. Henry Morgenthau, Jr. (1891-1967), U.S. Secretary of the Treasury (1934-45) ("Morgenthau, Henry, Jr."), had allowed the Treasury to purchase French gold at the usual fixed rate to keep the market supplied with dollars, thereby protecting the value of the franc ("U.S. Rescued Franc" 1). Louis XVI's dependence on foreign credit contributed to France's economic crisis in the years immediately preceding the Revolution of 1789 (Salvemini 85-110). Pound probably saw the two situations as analogous: in both cases he would perceive the international bankers thriving at the expense of the French people. The "Raffalovich papers" possibly refers to Arthur Raffalovich's last work, written with Yves Gutot, advocating adherence to the gold standard, or to Raffalovich's published works in general. Raffalovich (1853-1921) was a Russian-French economist, a financial agent in France for the Russian government, and an economic journalist appearing frequently in French economic journals ("Arthur Raffalovich").

4. Stephen Lausanne was editor-in-chief of *Le Matin* and wrote on economic subjects.

5. "L. Bloom" is Pound's punning reference to Leon Blum (1872-1950), the French socialist premier (1936-37, 1938) ("Blum"). The pun evokes Leopold Bloom, James Joyce's "Ulysses," who, like Blum, was Jewish.

6. William Aberhart (1878-1943), premier of Alberta, Canada (1935-43), introduced a social credit program based on the ideas of C. H. Douglas (Elliott). Cf. n1, above.

7. Clifford Hugh Douglas (1879-1952) was a British civil engineer and social economist whose theory of "social credit" was influential on Pound and others.

He was reconstruction advisor to Aberhart's government in Alberta in 1935 ("Douglas").

8. Larkin and Co., which operated nearly 200 department stores in Illinois, Pennsylvania, and New York, issued its own version of "private money" in the form of "merchandise bonds" (Pound, "An Impact" 149). "Young Larkin" was John N. Larkin, vice president and general manager of Larkin and Co. ("Larkins Buy Store in Chicago").

9. Sir Norman Angell (1872-1967) was an Anglo-American economist, journalist, and pacifist. He had been editor of *Foreign Affairs* (1928-31), author of works on international affairs, finance, and peace; and awarded the Nobel Peace Prize (1933) "Angell").

10. This may refer to Sir Henry Page Croft's proclaimed opposition to the proposed closing of the Suez Canal to Italian warships (Croft).

11. Sir Basil Zaharoff (1850-1936) was a British international financier who represented large munitions manufacturers during World War I ("Zaharoff"). His comings and goings were often shrouded in mystery.

12. Dexter Kimball (1865-1955) was an American economist and author (Edwards and Vasse 112). Pound is referring to his *Industrial Economics* (1929).

13. The reference is to Felix Frankfurter (1882-1965), then Harvard law professor and Roosevelt advisor, whom the President would appoint to the U.S. Supreme Court in 1939 ("Frankfurter"). The "Frankfurter/sausage" is Pound's way of referring to Roosevelt's Brain Trust.

9. Tinkham to Pound

> At
> Boston, Mass.,
> Twenty-six September,
> 1935

Mr. E. Pound
310 San Gregorio,
Venice, Italy

My dear Mr. Pound:
This is to acknowledge receipt of your communication
of September 2nd addressed to Congressman Tinkham. It has
been received by me, as Congressman Tinkham is absent upon a
vacation.

> Very truly yours,
> [signed] Gertrude Ryan
> Secretary to
> CONGRESSMAN TINKHAM

10.   Pound to Tinkham

My Dear Congressman Tinkham/ I send you this carbon, {in}
to reinforce note to Senator B/Hotel Italia
vide P.S.   ROME I oct 1935
                                                      XIII
The Hon
Wm Borah

My Dear Senator
                    Cngratulations on as much as has been quoted
of yr remarks on the league of Nations.[1]

                    The question of Abyssinia is NOT whether the
league wants etc/ or don't want.

                    It is a question of whether ANY nation that
doesn't crawl on its belly and take orders from London
        (from the most treacherous nation of earth) is
to have the league used against it; is to suffer unlimited
and unscrupulous blackmail, wangled by England.

Re/France, a recent issue of VU (no. 380; no date
on clippings sent me) contains an article on Bank of France
[by] Francis Delaisi,[2] which ought to be in the hands of every
senator and congressman who can read french.
                    Practically the first clear exposition of why
french politics are what they are, and why they have five
ministries in a week etc.

Tri/part treaties Eng/Fr/Ital re/ Abys/ did NOT
invite Abys/ to sign.

                    y:v:t:

The Hon Senator hasn't answered my letters since I expressed
{some} an estimate of H. Hoover, which I strongly suspect you
wd/ endorse in substance, if not in exposition.[3]

England wants the earth, and demands admiration for her
self-sacrifice while trying to get it.

1. William Edgar Borah (1865-1940), the U. S. Senator from Idaho (1907-40),
was an outspoken isolationist and opponent of the League of Nations. As he did

with Tinkham, Pound corresponded often with the Senator during the 1930s (Pearlman 419, 421).

2. Francis Delaisi (1873-1947) was a journalist, author, and economic reformer who was influential in French Leftist politics from before World War I through the interwar years. His two principal concerns—preventing a second European war and the nefarious influence of international finance—were shared by Pound. In Delaisi's view, the conspiracy of international finance was the chief villainy of modern capitalist society. It was the financiers (notably the Jewish ones) who controlled political as well as economic power, thereby giving the lie to democracy (Mazgaj 136-37, 245n). If workers were to survive under this plutocracy, they would have to study and emulate its industrial organization: "a technologically proficient, highly centralized capitalism could be successfully challenged only by a labor movement itself technologically proficient and highly centralized" (Mazgaj 136).

3. Pound is probably referring to his letter to Borah of 8 May 1934 (unpublished), in which he has this to say about the possibility of Hoover running again for president: "tell that fat cheater of chinamen that the only things about him that cd. run are his nose or his hemeroids [sic.]."

11. Tinkham to Pound

October 21, 1935

My dear Doctor Pound:

      The copy of your letter of October 1 to Senator Borah which you sent to Congressman Tinkham has been received in Mr. Tinkham's absence. Mr. Tinkham is now abroad and is not expected to return to the United States before the end of November. Your communication will be placed upon his desk for his attention.

Very truly yours,
[signed] G. C. Hamelin
Secretary to Mr. Tinkham

Doctor Ezra Pound
Hotel Italia
Rome, Italy

12.   Pound to Tinkham

27 Dec [1935]

The Hon. G.H. Tinkham

Dear Mr Tinkham

I shall enc/ a note to yr / glory from the
Corriere, if I can find a copy.[1]
Yesterday AT LAST a little mystery was cleared.
"Mr Eden, in 1923 married into the powerful banking family
of Beckett. Sir Gervase idem, director of Westminster bank.
In the same year master Tony entered Parliament for Warwick
and Leamington.
Nacherly hiz rize wuz rapid. The secrecy of brit.
diplomacy does not broadcast these simple causes of undesirable
effects.
If we consider Tony's "formation", Eton to start,
and a third son.
I probably never wrote to you a 14 year old Brit. school
boy denounced my poetry a couple of years ago because of
TRUTH it contained. A long quite sincere letter full
of outraged feeling, plus complete exposition of theory that
one must lie to keep up appearances, and that truth wd/
shatter society.
As a third son, Tony E/ wd. have been
brought up in luxury, but wd/ not INHERIT.
Haven't had time
to trace Sir Gervase particular bias/[2]
I have collected a little
information re/ Birmingham Small Arms, and Whitworth
Chemicals
as factors in what is and what is NOT
proper opinion in the British Press. I WISH the Nye
committee wd/ unbend a little and show a bit more curiosity.[3]

Did I send you the little story of the Jap
army corps that just wandered into somewhere and vanished?
It has NOT been broadcast. I am perhaps betraying a
confidence,
but I don't know to whom better.
I think both Japan and Germany have "enough to
do" and probably need a few rods, bowie knives and other
convenient implements.

(Statement to be recd. with due caution
and reserve.)
I wd. be honestly grateful for any indication you can give
me of what COMMON SENSE conservative opinion is re/
money,
its nature etc.
I know what the "advanced ideas are".
Landon[4] seems to me very ignorant. I take it some
recognition of new faculties for production MUST be made
    the issue of
in money and/or credit?
Whereto there is NO need of
shivvering the constitution or having the govt. blow the
nose and wash the ears of its citizens.
I have put the matter, during the past I5
years, with increasing frequency, to a number of responsible
men.
I may say that Dessari seems to me to think more clearly
than do several members of our own
cabinet (Have you perused Roper and the
elder Morgenthau on the "soul", or investigated the
leanings of Tugwell toward the Oxford (or Buckmanite)
movement?[5]
There is a chap named Peter Larranaga now in
the U.S. who has no reforming or messianic urge, but who has
written some very lucid things about economics.[6] I have no
idea what he is like personally. Understand he has built
some good roads. Might be useful in framing a SANE
monetary program, or at least one that ANY one of 200
younger writers on money couldn't show up as IDIOTIC.
I have been wrasTlin' with Mc N. Wilson, who
has some interesting remarks in "Defeat of Debt"[7] but has
that curious British tendency to identify the Reigning
incumbant of the White House with the late J. Christ of
Nazareth
and Jerusalem.
I hope somebody has jammed New Democracy for Dec. Ist. into
yr/
    mail box. Can't answer for anything but my one article.[8]

seasons greetings

[The following fragment is filed with this letter at the Beinecke
Library.]

I suppose it wd/ be quite irregular if not wholly impossible
to force the HOUSE to discuss principles?
Senator Cutting's confidential list of Senators and Congressmen
who understood something of the
subject was rather BRIEF.[9]
The original object of
legislature was not that of
educating its members AFTER
election;
but "our form of govt. is
fundamentally flexible".
Do the blighters KNOW
what (and/or) if they think?
And if so how many of 'em
wd/ have the courage or be
permitted to say so.

[Note: Pound had pro-
bably pasted something
here – perhaps Cutting's
"confidential list."]

1. Tinkham had been touring Europe and observing the political situation there
in the autumn of 1935. His public response was to criticize the Roosevelt
Administration for its support of League of Nations sanctions against Italy for its
attack on Abyssinia, and to recommend U. S. withdrawal from the Kellogg-
Briand Pact, which he considered an "alien" conception, a threat to U. S.
neutrality, and ironically, a means toward war ("Sees U. S. Approaching War";
"Tinkham Will Ask End of Peace Pact"). The "Corriere" was probably the
Corrière della Sera of Milan, which Mussolini "fascistized" in 1923 (Devendittis).
It probably reported on Tinkham's comments, no doubt applauding his
sentiments. Tinkham himself refers to his statement in Letter 17, 20 June 1936.
2. "Mr. Eden" and "Tony" are Robert Anthony Eden (1897-1977), the British
diplomat and politician who was minister without portfolio to the League of
Nations (1935), Foreign Affairs Secretary (1935-38), and Dominions Secretary
(1939) ("Eden"). The British financier Sir Gervase Beckett (1866-1937), in
addition to being a director of the Westminster Bank and father-in-law to Eden,
was chairman of the Yorkshire Post and owner/editor of The Saturday Review
("Gervase Beckett, English Banker"). To Pound, the family connection
suggested interlocking ties among government, finance, and media control that
were highly suspicious. The related references to Eton and the "Brit. school boy"
cast further doubt on Eden's character, the suggestion being that the English
private schools, where Eden's "formation" had begun, fostered a habit of
obfuscation.
3. Birmingham Small Arms was a British manufacturer of Daimler automobiles,
motorcycles, bicycles, and machine tools, in addition to small armaments
("Company Meetings"). Whitworth Chemicals was probably a subsidiary of
Vickers-Armstrong Ltd., which was the leading British armaments firm, and
which had taken over Armstrong-Whitworth, another armaments-related
company ("Vickers' Acquisition"). The Senate Munitions Investigating
Committee (the Nye Committee) had found ties between U. S. bankers and

Allied munitions makers before U. S. entry into World War I ("Nye"). Pound would have wanted the committee to look into the activities of both of these firms.

4. Alfred Mossman Landon (1887-1987), then governor of Kansas, would be the Republican presidential candidate in 1936 ("Landon").

5. I can find no information on "Dessari." Pound may have been thinking of the French writer and economic statistician, Jean Dessirier, who advocated devaluation in the French franc crisis (Jackson, Julian 115-16). Taking this position, Dessirier, like Pound, was in opposition to "Tannery's betrayal of France," which Pound refers to in Letters 8 and 18. See also Letter 8, n3. Daniel Calhoun Roper (1867-1943) was Secretary of Commerce (1933-38) ("Roper"). Henry Morgenthau, "the elder" (1856-1946) was an American diplomat who had served as a technical expert at the London Monetary and Economic Conference in 1933 ("Morgenthau, Henry"). Rexford Guy Tugwell (1891-1979) was an economic advisor to President Roosevelt and Undersecretary of Agriculture (1934-37) ("Tugwell"). I can find no information on Roper and Morgenthau on the "soul," nor on Tugwell's "Buckmanite" leanings.

6. Pedro J. Larranaga was a Peruvian member of the Inter-American Financial and Economic Advisory Committee and well known publicist and writer on social and economic issues. ("Peruvian is on Way Here").

7. Robert McNair Wilson was a British writer on many subjects, including money, economics, and Christianity. He was a correspondent for the London *Times*, but also contributed to smaller publications such as *The New English Weekly*, where Pound also frequently appeared (Terrell, vol. 2 681; Heymann 321).

8. The article to which Pound refers is his "Who Gets It?" published in *New Democracy*, December 1935 (Gallup C1275).

9. The reference is to Senator Bronson Cutting of New Mexico, with whom Pound carried on a substantial correspondence until the Senator's untimely death in an airplane crash (Pearlman 419). Cutting's "list," which he included in a letter to Pound dated 24 May 1934 (unpublished), was actually two lists. One consisted of Senators Borah, Bone, LaFollette, Wagner, Black, Wheeler, and Costigan; and Congressmen Kvale, Zionchek, Goldsborough, Patman, and Lewis. The other consisted of 12 additional Congressmen who had "mostly crank notions of their own, but could perhaps be converted." It is interesting to note that Cutting did not include Congressman Tinkham on either list.

13. Tinkham to Pound

January 22, 1936

<u>Personal</u>
My dear Professor Pound:

Your communication of December 27 was duly received. I thank you for it and for the information it contained.

I note particularly your statement: "I would be honestly grateful for any indication you can give me of what COMMON SENSE conservative opinion is re/money, its nature, etc."

There are many schools of thought in the United States, as you well know. The most conservative school of thought regards money as merely a measure of value and a medium of exchange, as an instrument of trade and not the production of wealth; and not wealth itself. Those of this school think that we should have a convertible currency based upon gold because gold, though not stable, is the most nearly stable metal in a free market. Of course, the market has not been free for several years, but manipulated.

With all good wishes, I remain
Sincerely yours,
[signed] GEORGE HOLDEN TINKHAM

14. Pound to Tinkham

[January or February, 1936]

Hon. G.H. Tinkham

Dear Mr Tinkham
                    Thanks for a straight answer (which I will
    not repeat, as you have headed it private.)
First half of yr/ answer I agree with.
2nd/ half I wd/ argue. Gold MEASURE, probably O.K.
                    convertability / re/ Reg/ McKenna's report to Midland
Bank
a few days ago. Where it appears to me he admits what
I have printed before now.
                                    ADEQUATE supply even more
important
than fixity of the unit (but ALL immoderate measures
,all measures that ride an idea (any idea) to death
are merely stupid.[1] Old laws crop up in new conditions, but
they crop up
                    perhaps unrecognized as themselves.
                                    //
Am not writing to inflict theory on you/ but for
                                    ITEM
Eden (hell take him) son in law of Gervase Beckett of
                            Westminster Bank
Rup/ Beckett chairman.
a director of this same bank Lord Cranbourne, who "joined the
bank in I933" has resigned to become Under Sec. for
League of Nations Affairs.
            That places Eden in a nice Frame of Sassoons and
Becketts
(wd/ take a bile specialist to follow all the crookedness
of perfice Albion/
                            and it is VERY slow/

tentative, let us say "openness to conviction."

McKenna and Midland Bank, comparatively clean R McK. dont
lie
ALL the time.
Possibilities re/ the connections of the Westminster to Sassoon
                    this is a bit *simpliste* but all I've got

to etc/etc/   for the moment.[2]
        At any rate keep an open eye. if you have
time.

I once in my younger days before I was interested, but
when I was in London had a little diagram of how
members of Asquith Cabinet had each betrayed each other
all round in a nice little circle.

                    sincerely yours

1. Reginald McKenna was chairman of the Midland Bank, which was the most unorthodox of Britain's "big five" banks. Pound is probably referring to McKenna's statement that "the misuse [i.e., hoarding] of gold has driven us to abandon the fixity of the external value of our currency for the far more important benefit of stable internal value" ("British Bank Head" 27). Pound had made a similar point in his "Impact" where he contends that the real value of money is convertible into commodities that people really want (146), and that the function of money is not to create wealth (hoarding), but "to get the goods from where they are to the people that need them" (154).
2. Rupert Beckett (d. 1955) was also chairman of the *Yorkshire Post* ("Rupert E. Beckett"); Lord Cranbourne was Robert Arthur James Cecil (1893-1972), who served as Eden's undersecretary for the League of Nations (1935-38) ("Cecil"); and "Sassoons" refers to the influential British banking family who, like the Becketts, had newspaper connections, specifically with the London *Observer* and the *Sunday Times* (Comay 363-64). Pound was both fascinated with and suspicious of the apparent "conspiracy" of government, financial, and newspaper interests. Cf. Letter 12, n2.

15.   Pound to Tinkham

[6 February 1936]

Hon. George Tinkham

Dear Mr Tinkham
                    Forgive my writing so soon again on thorny topic/
re/ Vandenberg etc/etc/[1]

Trouble with brain trust is that it was HALF BAKED/ grant the
Tugwell's may have MEANT well. None of 'em knew
ENOUGH.
Ignorance of a bloke like Warburg is appalling.[2]

Are any serious republicans interested in formulating a platform
ECONOMIC platform that will stand inspection. (I knote that
both Beckett and McKenna (one each) noted points made in
my Impact. I dont mean they have read it. But that these factors
are admitted.[3]
                    Keynes, hell take him, blathering trained seal.
(I have TALKED to him.) patient has small pox, and K/ is then
put
up to tell the world that "a slight nettle rash" etc.[4]

The CONSTITUTION is O.K.   plenty of room in it for decent
monetary system. And, really !! the attempt to conceal
things plainly stated at various epochs, say by Paterson when
starting the Bank of England or by Rotschild in I860. is too
stupid.[5] No form of government can go on as sheer fake
forever.

I dont care which "party" wins this autumn. But immense good
could be done by having a REAL issue, not a fake one
as in last English elections.
If the Republican party would simply demand a SERIOUS
enquiry into the known facts of credit and currency it
wd/ mean an immense advance. That is IF they meant it.

Discussion IN ITALY seems to me in healthier state than
elsewhere. Bottai, Rossoni, Farinacci all honestly WANT the
truth.[6]
        I dont believe an article like mine in the Vita Italiana
for Jan. could be published in any other country with
approval of man of cabinet rank.[7] Any number of people here

seriously interested in mechanism of government AS Jefferson's circle was I20 I40 years ago.

When I say a serious enquiry I mean one where people like Odon Por, C.H. Douglas and myself wd. get a chance to cross examine the Tugwells, Warburgs, Spragues, Warrens, etc. Larranaga knows a lot, but seems to be sold on idea that Public Works (concurrent with hyperusury) are an answer. Fack is the most reasonable Freiwirtschafter.[8] I cant make out that Bankhead really understood the subject when he proposed his stamp scrip bill.[9] The blighter wont write to anyone but Fack. {HHHHHHHHHH}

The Larkins, father and son, running a 20 million dollar business. can't be mere impractical idiots.[10]

Roosevelt is wonder, the way he has taken up EVERY damn wheeze that has been tried or proposed in England and found idiotic/ every economic FAD, is amazing.

Whether the country is lucky to have 'em tried
once and for all and done with, I dont know.

Doles! incitement to shiftlessness with concurrent PENALIZATION of everyone who is efficient or willing to be. bimentalism !!bi/carotism etc.

forgive this outbreak

I note in Chris/ Hollis "Two Nations" just out, Rutledge.[11] he talks about English prices, stable for two centuries (Hen VIII time) WHEN, damn, prices AS MEASURED IN METAL
were steadily declining through the whole period. And metal was the supposed measure. Marx and La Tour du Pin[12] couldn't think MONEY / and with most of the stabilization cranks we are up against people who WON'T think "MEASURE".

---

1. Arthur Hendrick Vandenberg (1884-1951) was the U. S. Senator from Michigan (1928-51) ("Vandenberg"). In the absence of a previous (extant) letter that could shed light, the "thorny topic" must remain a matter for speculation. However, judging from subsequent letters one might surmise that it had to do with a difference of opinion on Vandenberg's merits. Tinkham was a Vandenberg supporter; Pound was not. See Letters 38, 79, 81, and 89.
2. For note on Tugwell see Letter 12, n5. James Paul Warburg (1896-1969), American banker and author, had been financial advisor to the 1933 World

Economic Conference ("Warburg"). Both men were members of Roosevelt's Brain Trust.

3. I can find no specific point in Rupert Beckett's annual report to the Westminster Bank that is similar to anything in Pound's "Impact." However, the two texts do convey a common disapproval of the gold standard ("Company Meetings: Westminster Bank"; "Impact" 146, 149). For a note on McKenna's "point," see Letter 14, nl.

4. John Maynard Keynes (1883-1946) was the noted British economist. Pound may have considered him a "trained seal" of the financial interests because he advocated bank loans as the best means of financing public expenditures (Dillard 573).

5. William Paterson (1658-1719) was the chief founder of the Bank of England in 1694 (Edwards and Vasse 168). Mayer Amschel Rothschild (1744-1812) was the founder of the noted international banking family; his son, Nathan Mayer Rothschild (1777-1836), founded the London branch of the family in 1805 (Ricardo). What was "plainly stated" by Paterson when he founded the Bank of England was the basis for what Pound regarded as the Bank's usurious policy: "the bank hath benefit of the interest on all moneys which it creates out of nothing" (quoted in Pound, "A Visiting Card" 308; see also Canto 46). The Rothschild reference is probably to what one of the Rothschild brothers wrote, quoting Treasury Secretary John Sherman, in a letter to the New York firm of Ikleheimer, Morton and Van der Gould, dated 25 June 1863: "Those few who can understand the (usurocratic) system will be...busy getting profits,...while the general public...will probably never suspect that the system is absolutely against their interests" (quoted in Pound, "A Visiting Card" 311; see also Canto 46).

6. Giuseppe Bottai (1895-1959) held several posts in Mussolini's cabinet. In 1936 he was governor of Rome, Minister of National Education, and a member of the Fascist Grand Council (DeGrand, "Bottai"). Edmondo Rossoni (1884-1965) was Mussolini's Minister of Agriculture (1935-39) (Cannistraro, "Rossoni"). Roberto Farinacci (1892-1945), who hated Jews, Catholics, and socialists, was a member of the Fascist Grand Council (DeGrand, "Farinacci").

7. The article Pound refers to is "Moneta Fascista," published in the January/June issue of *La Vita Italiana* for 1936 (Gallup, C1281).

8. Odon Por (b. 1883) was a Hungarian-Italian economist and social critic who wrote much about Fascism. Like Pound, he was affiliated with *The New English Weekly* (Edwards and Vasse; Finlay 174). Oliver Mitchell Wentworth Sprague (1873-1953), a Harvard economist, had been financial advisor to the Bank of England, liaison officer between the Bank and foreign capitals, member of the League of Nations committee on the purchasing power of gold, chairman of the committee on gold supply, and financial advisor to the U. S. government ("Many Years at Harvard"). In 1936 he was president of the American Economic Association ("Learned Societies Elect"). George Frederick Warren (1874-1938) was an American agricultural economist and financial advisor to Roosevelt. He advocated a "commodity dollar," a monetary unit whose gold content would fluctuate with prices; this concept influenced the government's gold-buying policy from October 1938 ("Warren"). Hugo Fack was the American publisher of Silvio Gesell (see Letter 41, n5) and the monthly, *The Way Out* (Pound, "An Introduction" 183). A "Freiwirtschafter" is a proponent of a free market economy. For notes on C. H. Douglas and Larranaga, see Letter 8, n7, and Letter 12, n5.

9. John Hollis Bankhead (1872-1946) was U. S. Senator from Alabama (1931-46) ("Bankhead, John Hollis"). On 11 March 1933 he introduced his stamp-scrip bill to the Committee on Banking and Currency. On the same day Congressman Pattengill introduced a similar bill in the House. Both bills died in committee. On 30 March 1933 Senator Bankhead tried again with a stamp-money amendment to a relief bill, but the amendment was rejected. Then, on 13 April 1933, he introduced a resolution urging the Senate Banking Committee to investigate a number of methods to change the currency system to increase commodity prices and restore normal debt-paying power. Stamp money was just one of the methods he suggested. The committee never reported on this resolution. (*Cong. Rec.* 11 Mar. 1933: 3336-39; 30 Mar. 1933: 1027-35; 13 Apr. 1933: 1625).

10. See Letter 8, n8.

11. Christopher Hollis was a British biographer and economist ("To Teach at Notre Dame").

12. Marquis de la Tour du Pin (1834-1924), a French socialist and syndicalist, was the main theorist of the Catholic social movement at the end of the 19th century (Read 259-60).

16.   Pound to Tinkham

II March [1936]

The Hon. Geo. H. Tinkham
Washington D.C.

Dear Mr Tinkham
                    I am for "Tinkham 1940". And I am not
writing this letter frivolously. I am not interested in
impossibilities and I believe I have for months carried on
a more searching correspondence with the best economists than
anyone else has had the gumption to attempt.
                    I have been on the job for I8 years, and
I2 years ago I came here (Italy) to see the difference
between what blokes write in a high brow weekly and what
gets DONE.
                    Most writers on econ/are laboratory men. They
make blue prints, and have NO imagination. I mean they do
NOT
visualize humanity, Bill, Joe, and Henry DOING the things
on the program.
                    Most of 'em cant use WORDS. I mean they
do not start by defining their terms, and continue by
sticking to CLEAR definitions.
                    One of the most lucid of 'em, and a man
who is READ by govt. advisors has just written me
    "credit is debt"
                    Oh yeah, and east is west, and left is right.
Sure, he MEANS something, But by the time he has uttered
it isn't there.
                    ANOTHER CASE
                    Peeke,[1] I think the bloke's name is, writes
a buttery article about F.D.R. contribution to the "pure
science of mathematics"
                    and suddenly shifts from talking about
NUMBERS (arithmetic) to dollars.
                    Hollis[2] writes of prices being STABLE for two
centuries when prices were steadily declining AS MEASURED
in
metal. which was what they thought they were measuring by.

The job of building up a clean terminology GOES ON. We've
got
plenty of high brow magazines and Butchart's "MONEY" is

a start for a new library. Butch. Being the second generation
brought up, as you may say, By Orage, E.P. and Douglas.[3]
Daladier, Duboin (of Ligue du Droit du Travail)
Rossoni, Kozul in Jugoslavia, Hen. Ford recently, and EVEN
Hitler in one clause of his last outbreak all see certain
FACTS.[4]
If it were a mere matter of laboratory work, I wdn't
be
impelled to buy the postage stamp on this letter.
I am now after what you and Bill Borah can DO.
If, that is, you are interested, and want a program that will
WORK.
I don't know what you think of Borah. Hoover is a
crook
and the other possible candidates for 1936 are DEAD and
petrified
from the neck up.
The problem in dynamics is Tinkham 1940. IF
G.H.T. will consider sane monetary reform WITHIN the frame
of
the Constitution.
and without LOWERING anyone's standard of
living.
(though that phase of it [sic] question is probably above and
outside popular politics.)
You'd probably have to nominate Borah.[5] YOU, and not the
expansive Wm B. wd. have to make terms. That is to say YOU
wd/have to put the DEFINITE ideas into him. or make him
sign 'em.
There is no use in expecting any great precisions
from him.
(At least damn'd if I see it.)
//
On my part it means working on private letters to you
rather than in splashing ideas over printed pages.
I don't mean I wd. quit publishing economic articles,
but there wd/have to be coordination, and the mere pleasure of
uttering ideas, wd. have to be fitted into the probable
effect of printing them.
Lenin saw Mussolini as the one man who cd/
get anything DONE in Italy.
It is the Boss's genius for seeing what must be
day by day. What done FIRST. March 1936/what done next
after that April; May, June.
That is the kind of thought (or imagination

to use a word which Napoleon occasionally found useful) which is needed.

//

Borah election or non-election etc. needn't mean postponing a sane economic reform. There is no reason why you shouldn't come in 1940, emeritus, on the gratitude FOR having got it done.

/

If the press has gone short on reporting the Bank Reform here, you can get the general outline from my "Jefferson and/or Musso

lini). American edtn. P. 117 (same in Eng/edtn. Chap. XXX)
        state of Bank of the U.S. under Washington. Before Hamilton and Biddle had got in their dirty work.
              (lines following "While the govt. remained at Philadelphia".)[6]
For the Republican party to DO anything, the sole chance is a combination on the lines of Van Buren Jackson.[7]
                          You wd/have
to supply the Van B//element, the sharp definition of ideas.
              No use my putting down details UNLESS you approve at
least part of this letter.

[no closing]

1. "Peeke" probably refers to George Nelson Peek (1873-1943), who had been head of the Agricultural Adjustment Administration briefly in 1933, but was removed because of policy disagreements with Henry Wallace. Subsequently, he became a bitter critic of the New Deal ("Peek"). The "man who is READ by govt. advisors" is probably John Maynard Keynes (cf. Letter 15, n4; and "Bukos," the "economist consulted of nations," in Canto 101 [Klinck]).
2. Christopher Hollis (see Letter 15, n11).
3. Montgomery Butchart was a British economist whose book *Money* is a compendium of three centuries of thought on the nature of money and credit (Pound, "Introductory Textbook" 160). Alfred Richard Orage (1873-1934), a British journalist, was editor of the social credit publication, *New Age*. For note on Douglas, see Letter 8, n7.
4. Eduard Daladier (1884-1970), the statesman and Radical Party leader, had been and would be again the French prime minister (1933, 1934, 1938-40) ("Daladier"). Jacques Duboin, a well known economic publicist in France during the 1930s, popularized the "theory of abundance," which held that the economic crisis resulted from underconsumption, which itself arose from the unemployment caused by industrial mechanization (Jackson, Julian 16). Kozul was the Yugoslavian Minister of Building (Pound, unpublished letter to Borah, 12 March 1936). For note on Rossoni, see Letter 15, n6.

5. Senator Borah had been widely considered as a contender for the Republican Presidential nomination, but at the June convention in Cleveland Tinkham did not nominate him. Although Borah did receive 19 votes on the first ballot, Landon won the nomination unanimously on the second (*National Party Conventions* 82).

6. The entire passage from *Jefferson and/or Mussolini*, beginning with a quote from Thomas Jefferson, reads as follows:

> While the government remained at Philadelphia a selection of members of both Houses were constantly kept as directors who, on every occasion interesting to that institution, or to the *views of the federal head* voted at the will of that head; and together with the stockholding members, could always make the federal vote that of the majority.
>
> This was the bank in Federal hands, i.e., opposed to Jefferson, but an "engine of" Hamilton during Washington's administration. That is to say: during the first administrations there was *national control* of the *national finances*. This ceased when the administration changed WITHOUT there being a corresponding change in the control of the bank.
>
> Thereafter the fights against the First and Second Banks of the U. S. were fights to keep the control of the nation's finance out of control by a clique and to attain the use of the national resources for the benefit of the whole nation. (117)

7. The Jackson and Van Buren administrations of the 1830s fought to keep the control of the nation's finances out of the hands of private bankers. This is precisely what Pound wanted from a Tinkham-Borah administration.

17. Tinkham to Pound

June 20, 1936

<u>Personal</u>

My dear Doctor Pound:

I hope you will excuse the delay in my answering your very flattering communication of March 11. It was received at a time when I was under unusual pressure and shortly thereafter, when it would in ordinary circumstances have been brought to my attention, the work of my office was placed in some confusion by the absence of my secretary, on account of illness.

I always read your letters with the deepest interest, and am always delighted to hear from you.

It is now my intention to sail for Europe early next month and I am seriously thinking of coming to Italy. If I should, I shall give myself the pleasure of communicating with you.

Recently, I was informed that the gun which I fired against the Austrians at Capo d'Argine on the Piave River, on December 11, 1917, which was the first gun to be fired by an American after the declaration of war against Austria, has been placed in the War Museum at Rome. I should like to see it.

Last winter I gave a statement to the press here in which I said that the United States should not be a "puppet" state of Great Britain.[1] This statement was printed in Italy and was read by the Colonel of the battery with which I happened to be on December 11, 1917 when the United States declared war against Austria, and he wrote me of the incident to which I referred above. He is Doctor Giovanni Ravagli, Lieutenant Colonel of Auxiliary Artillery and Superior Inspector of Demesne, and his address is Villa Piancarelli, Pescara, Italy. In the summer he is at Teramo. I hope to see him also if I come to Italy.

Mussolini certainly has had a great triumph and in his age and generation is a great man. Any man who can successfully defy England and the League of Nations, representing fifty-two nations, is a man of strength and he has my admiration.

With cordial regards and with every good wish, I remain

Sincerely yours,

[signed] GEORGE HOLDEN TINKHAM

Doctor Ezra Pound
via Marsala 12-5
Rapallo, Italy

1. In his statement to the press, Tinkham had claimed that the Administration's neutrality bill then being considered by the House Foreign Affairs Committee, of which he was a member, gave the President too much power, increased the chances of war, and made "the United States a puppet state of Great Britain and a subsidiary of the League of Nations" ("House Gets Report").

18.   Pound to Tinkham

[26 June 1936]

BRAVO !
   Yesterday's postcard due to notices in Italian
press/clipping from Time, Feb. I5 just in. That's TALKIN' !!!¹

And to develop. I suspect that blighter Phillips is the new
nigger in Mr Hull's woodshed.²
BUT I come back to Tannery's betrayal of France/³ {we} NO
Straus
cd/resist the massed spendours of the Rothschilds.
It ain't HUMAN. Gheez (if you will pardon the divigation
for curial speech) I once took my dearly beloved publisher
Mr Liveright to a party in Paris and the EFFECT of the
splendours due to foreclosing on etc/etc//waaaaal,
I can picture Mr Straus showing young Morgenthau round
etc.⁴
          and I can not picture the American people of so different
origin, or the French people having a stand in.
          And Sieff lunches with Rothschild,⁵ and that
30% loan "from" London, with nothing moved, not a brass
farden
sent over to the frogs.
                    this grape vine (such as Ben Franklin saw wd/
come into existence.
          I haven't the exact next length in hand
but it all means ENTANGLEMENT in European affairs.
     with corresponding European tentacles heaven knows where
in
the U.S.
          The U.S. Treasury ought NOT to be in French politics,
french INTERNAL politics.

DeWendel's holdings in Mitsui ??? how much are they now?⁶
Can't remember if I sent you Delaisi's map of the French
rule? "VU" no 380 must be in congressional library anyhow.
     26/June I936

As for England, I want the connection ?? Sieff, Eden.
nothing exact yet.
But Eden, son in law Gervaise Beckett, Westminster Bank.
Cranbourne, a director of same bank, succeeds Eden as Sec? for
League. Sieff certainly in touch Paris Rothschild. supposed bank

hand behind Rothermere.[7] I dont KNOW.
                              personal testimony is that he [is a]
nasty piece of work. ANYHOW.

Zaharoff's whereabouts reported unknown. AND at his age...
       marrrrvelous...[8]

I keep on recommending Chapter XXX (as it is all Jefferson
and I dont have to be modest about authorship) of my

Jefferson and/or Mussolini.[9]

As NO news about Daladier gets printed in England, I think
anything you cd/do to get his views printed, widely
distributed in the U.S.A. wd. help toward American
independence.
The really appalling difficulty with getting America FREE from
British propaganda is that all Garrison Villard's {gann}
gang, all these sham highbrows and paste = liberals GOT
their IDEAS out of British coacoa papers/AND the next
generation, Wood Krutches, etc; GO ON DOING now, after
a quarter of a century.[10]
                      It used to be possible to transmit a TINY
stream of acid from France, as counter irritant, but
France was simply knocked out I914/I9.
Nothing but little papers with hardly more than private
circulation
except when Delaisi breaks into big circulation.

I go on reviewing occasional french books, but they are NOT
hammered down hard.
                      NO USE our expecting foreign intelligentzia
to save us. At least we oughtn't to go on expecting it.
//The enc/ review/might be of interest. I mean the
CONTRAST of
Italian reviewer going for root idea, and one that Morgan[11]
wd/ consider dangerous/
                      whereas that ass Nicolson (Harold) M/P[12]
merely slithered, and wdn't face Jeff's ideas/
He revd. the book in London Sunday Observer.
Much closer thought here than in Eng/ Spirito going for
Rossoni in detail and Rossoni printing it in his own paper.[13]
Much healthier atmosphere at least in some circles here
than in equally high spheres in England.
                      very truly yours

1. Pound must be referring to an article in *Newsweek*, not *Time*, on 15 February 1936. The *Newsweek* article mentions Tinkham's appearance before the Nye Committee, particularly his demand for investigations of Colonel Edward Mandell House, for his alleged unpatriotic sentiments and his alleged role in getting the U.S. involved in the World War; ambassador Walter Hines Page, for his "traitorous" behavior in England during the war; and the British "domination" of the U.S. State Department ("Guns" 10). The only mention of Tinkham in *Time* for 1936 was on 6 April in a note about Tinkham's refusal to move from his apartment in the Arlington Hotel, which had been rented by Tugwell's Resettlement Administration. Tinkham had claimed he had taken a lifetime lease on the apartment and refused to be "resettled" ("People" 72).

2. William Phillips (1878-1968), a career diplomat, was U.S. minister to Italy (1936-41). Cordell Hull (1871-1955) was Secretary of State (1933-44).

3. Cf. Letter 8, n3.

4. Horace Brisbin Liveright (1886-1933) had been Pound's publisher at Boni and Liveright, which he founded in 1918 (Edgett). Jesse Isidor Straus (1872-1936), a member of the department store family, had been president of Macy's, which had been long established in Paris. In 1933 Roosevelt had appointed him ambassador to France, a post he held until just before his death (Harlow). For notes on Morgenthau and the Rothschilds, see Letter 8, n3, and Letter 15, n5.

5. At the time of Pound's writing, Israel Moses Sieff (1889-1972) was vice chairman and joint managing director of Marks and Spenser Ltd., a British department store chain established in 1926 by his brother-in-law, Lord Marks. Sieff was also chairman of a political research group (P.E.P), from which position he was influential on British social and economic policy, and an active zionist (Marks & Spenser Ltd.; "Sieff"). "Rothschild" probably refers to Baron Edouard Alphonse James de Rothschild (1868-1949), the head of the French branch of the Rothschild banking family and chief regent of the Bank of France in 1936 ("Rothschild...," *Obituaries*).

6. François de Wendel (1874-1949), a French industrialist and political leader, was president of *La Comité des Forges*, the industrial trust ("Wendel"; cf. Letter 3, n4). Mitsui was a Japanese bank. For note on Delaisi, see Letter 10, n2.

7. Harold Sidney Harmsworth, 1st Viscount Rothermere (1868-1940) was a British newspaper publisher ("Harmsworth"). For note on Cranbourne, see Letter 14, n2. Also, cf. Letter 12, n2, on Eden et. al.

8. For note on Zaharoff, see Letter 8, n11.

9. Cf. Letter 16, n6.

10. Oswald Garrison Villard (1872-1949) was an American editor and author who had been connected with the New York *Evening Post* and *The Nation* ("Viilard"). Joseph Wood Krutch (1893-1970) was an American author, educator, and social and literary critic ("Krutch").

11. John Pierpont Morgan (1837-1913), the American banker and financier.

12. Harold Nicolson (1886-1968) was a British diplomat, politician, and journalist ("Nicolson").

13. Ugo Spirito (1896-1968) was an Italian philosopher interested in economics and the corporate state. His brand of Fascism had a "communist" bent in that he saw corporate ownership passing from stockholders to producers, whose proprietorship would be based on technical expertise (Cannistraro, "Spirito"). For note on Rossoni, see Letter 15, n6.

19. Tinkham to Pound

ROME, September 8, 1936

Professor Ezra Pound,
Via Marsala 12-5
Rapallo.
My dear Professor:
I arrived Saturday September 5th in
Rome and I am staying at the Excelsior
Hotel. I shall probably remain around
Rome until about the 20th of September.
I thought being so near you I should send
you a letter of greeting with my compli-
ments.
With kindest personal regards and
best wishes, I am
Sincerely yours,
[signed] George Holden Tinkham

20. Pound to Tinkham

[10 September 1936]

310 San Gregorio
VENICE

Dear Mr Tinkham
Thanks for yr/letter. I "just can't"
get to Rome now but nobody ought to visit Italy
(even if it is for the seventeenth time) without passing
through Venice.
ANY chance of your making it? No big game
here for you to shoot, only one unfortunate lion, but
you might shoot the responsible parties for putting the animal
in a cage that is MUCH too small.

At any rate if I can't see you do please see Odon Por.
address 4 via Ugo Bassi

He can tell you more about economics than anyone else in
Europe, though I have had some extremely interesting
news in the last few days. Most of which gets to Por
but I cant elaborate it. At any rate if you pass
through England you might also see Hollis and R. McKenna[1]
The news comes too fast to deal with in
private letters. Certain fakes are too well known NOW to last
much longer.
Hope your itinerary takes in this
lagumar village.
cordially

1. For notes on Por, Hollis, and McKenna, see Letter 15, n8 and n11, and Letter
14, n1.

21.   Tinkham to Pound

ROME, September 15, 1936.

Professor Ezra P. Pound [*sic*],
    310 San Gragorio,
        Venice.
My dear Professor:
    Your communication of September 10 has been
duly received and I was most pleased to hear
from you. Odon Por, Esquire, called upon me in
Rome and gave me your compliments. I had a
very interesting conversation with him.
    I am coming to Venice leaving Rome by plane
at 7:30 a.m. Saturday. I shall stop at the
Excelsior Hotel at the Lido. I shall stay Saturday, Sunday, Monday, and Tuesday at Venice going
Monday and Tuesday by automobile to Capo d'Argine
where I fired the first American gun on December
11, 1917 after the United States had declared war
against Austria. I then intend to go to the
place on the top of Monte Grappa where my staff
limousine was destroyed in artillery action.
    I shall sail Thursday on the Rex from
Genoa. You may be sure I will communicate with
you.
    With kindest personal regards and best
wishes, I am
                Sincerely yours,
          [signed] George Holden Tinkham

1. For note on Odon Por see Letter 15, n8.

22. Pound to Tinkham

310 San Gregorio
VENEZIA
Italy
25 Sept. anno XIV
[1936]

G.C. Hamelin
Dear Miss Hamelin
I have just seen Mr Tinkham, and he wishes you to send me a copy of his 8000 word speech against COMMUNISM.
Please send it to this address.[1]

I shd. like copies of any other speeches of his, if you have spare copies <u>handy</u>
yours very truly
Ezra Pound

1. Pound comments on Tinkham's "communism" speech in his letter of 23 October 1936 (see Letter 27).

23. Tinkham to Pound

October 9, 1936

My dear Doctor Pound:

      In compliance with the request contained in your letter of September 25, received this morning, I am sending to you herewith a copy of Mr. Tinkham's speech in the House of Representatives on May 14, 1935.[1]

      At the moment, Mr. Tinkham's regular office is closed for repairs. Upon my return there, I shall see if there are any other speeches available in which you might be interested.

Very truly yours,
[signed] G.C. Hamelin
Secretary to Mr. Tinkham

Doctor Ezra Pound
310 San Gregorio
VENEZIA, ITALY

encl.

1. Pound responds in his letter of 23 October 1936 (see Letter 27).

24. Pound to Tinkham

11 Oct. anno XIV [1936]
310 San Gregorio   VENEZIA

Dear G.H.T.

         1. I hope the tubing and piping is O.K., if
eating
it breaks out again try a FEW drops of Vapex on a
lump of sugGAR. I mean a FEW, dont try swallowing the
whole bottle neat.

         2.   I sure did enjoy your week in Venice.
3. As soon as, or IF the North American Review prints
my note on Jefferson, I shall try opening 'em up on
American form of government.
              (New English Weekly shd/ print
a note on "Race" in their next issue.)

As PRACTICAL program for return to U.S. system in
form that wd. be EFFICIENT now.[1]

I. Senate and House debates shd/ be broadcast.
           That is up to date, and only way
people can find out who is in congress.

2. Wd. you consider proposing it/ AND a further
reform re/ committees.[2] That is House shd/ be divided
into somewhat larger committees than at present.

I dont know how long House now sits. But say it works
theoretically four hours a day. Two hours shd. be
in these separate committees, or even three, and full
assembly only for final speeches and voting.
Instead of possibly vague system and seniority rules
the committees shd. each contain ONE representative from
the 20 larger states, and one from groups of smaller
states, grouped by mutual agreement and having
similar interests.

This preserves the 1789 form, but has some of the
advantages of new Italian program where [in] the grand council
every man is supposed to be represented by someone of
his own trade.
The arguments in committee shd. be all (or ?? largely)

printed, as the Congressional record now is. Votes in
House shd. occur only after members have had chance
(I dont say they wd. TAKE it, but shd. have chance to
read the committee proceedings.)

This system wd. allow real debate on MORE issues than
can possibly be dealt with in full house.

I see no chance for parliamentary govt. or whatever
congressional govt. is supposed to be, unless INTEREST
in congress is resurrected.
There is NO reason why all information shd. get to
White House before the legislature has a chance at it.

   This strike you as reasonable?
Hope you will soon hear from Butch.[3]
I enc. two cards that happen to be on my desk. (writing on them
contains nothing private.) one of Santa Maria Miracoli, and
the other a view of Rapallo (hope you will verify photographer's
opinion, after you get enough Pacific Ocean.)
                    [no closing]

1. *The North American Review* would print Pound's article, "The Jefferson-
Adams Correspondence," in August 1937; his article "Race" was published in
The New English Weekly on 15 October 1936. While the "note on Jefferson" is
"an attempt to show how [the Jefferson-Adams correspondence] might serve as a
point of departure...for a revalorization of our cultural heritage" (especially as it
descends intellectually from the French encyclopedists) (315-16), the "Race"
article is more pertinent in the present context because it suggests the
"PRACTICAL programs" Pound refers to. The gist of the article is contained in
the opening paragraphs:

> Communism is Muscovite, Socialism is German and embodies the worst
> defect of that race, democracy with representation divided in respect to
> geographic areas is Anglo-American, and the Corporate State is Latin.
>   Resistance to any one of these modes of government by races whereto it
> is alien, is a sign of health, submission to any one of them by a race whereto it
> is alien is a sign of decay. (12)

Tinkham would have been particularly interested in this article as he considered
himself a specialist on racial traits and comparative ethnology (McKee 302).
2. Tinkham did not raise any of these issues in Congress.
3. "Butch" is Montgomery Butchart (see Letter 16, n3).

25. Tinkham to Pound

Paris, France, October 17, 1936.

Ezra Pound, Esquire,
   via Marsala 12-5,
      Rapallo, Italy.

My dear Mr. Pound:

Your communication of October 11 I received while here in Paris. As I am under a good deal of time pressure, I will not answer it at length.

I was much pleased to hear from you. I leave Paris to-morrow, Sunday, October 18, for London, and sail for the United States on the 28th of October.

When I arrived at Bucharest, I had a doctor and a nurse and went to bed with bronchitis. At the end of ten days I recovered, and I am in an excellent form now.

I desire to thank you very much for all your courtesies and attention while I was at Venice. Had I not had you, I should have been deprived of a great deal of pleasure. All of the places you took me to were little "gems" which I never should have seen.

Thanking you, and with high regards, I remain.

Sincerely yours,
[signed] George Holden Tinkham.

26. Pound to Tinkham

[Between 11 and 23 October 1936]
still Venice, but leaving
                              address
                                      via Marsala 12/5
                                              RAPALLO

Dear Uncle George
                    (Is that {addre} form of address of
{n} any political use?)
                        I will suppress it in private
correspondence if yr/ secretaries misinterpret it.[1]

I hope you will see my article in NEW ENGLISH WEEKLY
for 15th oct.[2]

(there is a misplaced comma, and a verb misprinted.)

I have just bet myself six pence, that Landon
will git licked. And have written a few pages on
why that is as it shd/ be.
                            If I am wrong I can tear up
the article.
I am saying that congress cd/ revive by immediately
demanding an enquiry into money, its nature and mode
of issue.
If you want to originate this, I can hold the article.
I want you to lead/ and will follow as ordered.

But I am, nacherly ready to bust out, unauthorized,
and in way that cant possibly imply any collusion.[3]
                        [no closing]

1. This letter marks the first instance, as far as I know, of Pound's using "Uncle
George" in reference to Tinkham.
2. The article here referred to is "Race"; cf. Letter 24, n1.
3. For Pound's article on Landon, see "Landon, or the Loser" in *New English
Weekly*, 16 November 1936, 105-06 (Gallup, C1378).

27. Pound to Tinkham

23 Oct/ [1936]

Dear Uncle George
            What I like best about yr/ speech on Russia is
that you go straight to ROOT. Dictatorship of proletariat/
That's it/ Trap to get people out of one tyranny into another.

            Speech O.KAY: but...communism is a disease
which attacks weakened organisms.

            Demand for withdrawal of Russia
proper. Dont think I dont see the value of yr/ attack
as formal move.[1]
            BUT the only way to keep OUT some such
mould and rot is to CURE the economic system.

Coughlin has some useful quotations from Jackson etc.
in his book "Money"

            I dont refer to anything but the quotations
at the back of it.[2]

+2
I hope you have collected some information in Paris/
and that you will see several people in London.

3
re / U.S.A.
            Young Jas. Laughlin[3] writes me very sensible letters
as per sample
            "You see, boss, America is not like what you
think it is. There is nobody here who is interested in taking
life as seriously as you do."

            Followed by a few concrete examples. It appears that Pell[4]

            edtr. North American Review is 30; thinks Social Credit
or
Mussolini or anything like that is crap.
                        [no closing]

1. In the *Congressional Record* the headnote to Tinkham's speech of 14 May 1935 reads as follows:

> Undisputed evidence from Russian and American sources shows that the Union of Soviet Socialist Republics promotes activities to undermine the institutions of the United States and to overthrow its government in complete repudiation of the pledges which it gave to obtain United States recognition.

Because of this situation, as he perceived it, Tinkham recommended severing diplomatic relations with Russia and even called for an inquiry into the possible impeachment of Government officials who were responsible for the state of affairs on the grounds of not upholding their oath to defend the Constitution (*Cong. Rec.* 14 May 1935: 7526-34).

2. Father Charles Edward Coughlin (1891-1979) was an American Roman Catholic priest who attacked the New Deal in print and over the radio. His views became increasingly anti-semitic and pro-fascist until he was silenced by his superiors in 1942 ("Coughlin"). I can find no record of his book, "Money." Pound may have been thinking of his *Money, Questions and Answers*, published in 1936, and may have confused the title with Montgomery Butchart's book, *Money*, which he mentions in Letter 16.

3. James Laughlin was a young literature student who visited Pound at Rapallo during the 1930s. He became a Pound protege, editing the literary section of *New Democracy*. He later used the title of his column, "New Directions," for the name of his publishing company. New Directions became Pound's principal publisher (Stock 322-23).

4. John Pell had been editor of *The North American Review* since spring 1935.

28. Pound to Tinkham

[October 1936]

Dear G.H.T.
This will probably miss you in London; but there was one
question of yrs/ which I didn't answer in Venice

I didn't quite get what you were driving at, and the question
is not one to answer straight off anyone's bat, and without
qualification.

You asked: will the price of gold go up?

The answer is generically: YES, and I dont give a damn if it
does.

Of course it wont go up at a specific moment, and it wont
go up IF you have all sorts of monkeyings; govt. etc.
that wont let it / etc.

But suppose that after 20 years of various wangles one did
emerge into a free market; in say 1960.

Unless some chemist had managed to make
synthetic gold etc.
gold wd. I think be UP as against
monetary units.

It wd. be very much up against manufactured
products IF any sense of reality underlay the public mentality
(which is doubtful.. I mean has the pubk. got ANY)

The thing to eliminate is a bottle = neck. The strangling of
exchange.

The nature fakers focus on foreign exchange. Sheer smoke
screen
to keep mind off internal or 90% + of trade. in U.S.

I am thinking of a modus vivendi with; say; Og Mills[1] (damn
him).
For people at that level of intelligence I think the
answer is: the price of gold will go up (e v e n t u a l l y

after as much short term wobble and fluctuation as the old gang can get past the police.

So will chinese jade for collectors. At least the better quality of ancient carved jade.

During the next I6 years
The fun of playing with gold will probably depend much more on inside tips about legislative action than it will on knowledge of market for merchandise etc.

Man might put a couple of gold bricks in the cellarage for his great grandchildren; and let himself and sons starve in the interim.

Private holding might be illegal, though hardly for bullion,
certainly not for unmined gold.
UNLESS mineral
wealth were nationalized, or farmed to concessionaires
...that has happened before.
latter   Persian petrol etc.

The timid and the seekers for absoLOOT safety might just as well die ANYhow.

Main curve of gold over say a century will be UP.

And the price of wheat: meat and clothing is more important in national economy.

sorry to be so dull; but hope this is clear/ or at least that it exposes my mental nakedness.

Delaisi or Duboin[2] has got round to remarking that the distance from Paris to Dijon will not be altered by shortening the kilometer.
In fact several of the ideas in my Volitionist 8 questions formulated I933, are now crawling into French print

the 4th is the sticker.[3]   devme//

1. Ogden Livingston Mills (1884-1937) was undersecretary of the U. S. Treasury (1927-32) and Secretary of the Treasury (1932-33) ("Mills").

2. For notes on Francis Delaisi and Jacques Duboin, see Letter 10, n2, and Letter 16, n4.

3. In August 1934 Pound had a list of eight questions about economics printed up and then sent them to bankers, economists, politicians, and others, requesting that they reply. The form was headed "Volitionist Economics," and contained the following "questions":

> Which of the following statements do you agree with?
>
> 1. It is an outrage that the state shd. run into debt to individuals by the act and in the act of creating real wealth.
>
> 2. Several nations recognize the necessity of distributing purchasing power. They do actually distribute it. The question is whether it shd. be distributed as favour to corporations; as reward for not having a job; or impartially and per capita.
>
> 3. A country CAN have one currency for internal use, and another good both for home and foreign use.
>
> 4. If money is regarded as certificate of work done, taxes are no longer necessary.
>
> 5. It is possible to concentrate all taxation onto the actual paper money of a country (or onto one sort of its money).
>
> 6. You can issue valid paper money against any commodity UP TO the amount of that commodity that people want.
>
> 7. Some of the commonest failures of clarity among economists are due to using one word to signify two or more different concepts: such as, DEMAND, meaning sometimes WANT and sometimes power to buy; authoritative, meaning also responsible.
>
> 8. It is an outrage that the owner of one commodity can not exchange it with someone possessing another, without being impeded or taxed by a third party holding a monopoly over some third substance or controlling some convention, regardless of what it be called. (quoted in Stock, *Life* 321-22)

Pound's purpose in soliciting responses to these "questions" was not merely to take a poll, but to determine the "basis of agreement between various schools of contemporary economics" (unpublished letter to Morgenthau Sr.).

29.   Pound to Tinkham

4 Nov [1936]

Dear Mr Tinkham
                    Judging from first radio reports that PORE
OLE
EFFERLUNT aint got nothink but hiz tail left to stand on.
If it weren't for the delay in mail I wd/ hold off for a
                    as
few days; but this wont reach you before the I5th.
I proceed.

            A party responsible for Hoover getting into the White
House; deserves to die. and that wasn't the first offense,
though it was the worst.

                    The same wd. apply to Col. House.[1]

This is really a WAIL for guidance. Can you check up on
the following questions and items.
I.   Has the old guard learned ANYTHING by the election; or

            do they still think the peepul WANt a dictatorship
            from the DuPonts and Wall St. with the hired Atlantic
            Monthly bleating behind it?

2.   Do they NOW admit that a policy of sheer intellectual

            cowardice/ with a stuffed non = entity at head of ticket
            wont work?

            A man who knows NOTHING, who dont even know
enough
            to stall with efficiency to conceal his ignorance!

I mean IS the question of a soft westerner OUT for I940
or are there still simps/ wd. need to be TOLD about that.

ARE the following safe planks that can be agreed on:

            THE CONSTITUTION (including the clause that
                congress had the right to coin money and
[distribute] it legally; despite Eccles and Barney Baruch.[2]

Non intervention in Europe. Monroe doctrine.
//
Is there any better IMMEDIATE way of attack than that of
demanding a thorough investigation of the nature of MONEY?
              attacking the socialistic FOLLIES by that
investigation.

Linc Steffens[3] once said to me: Can't do anything with
revolution =
aries until they are at the END
                    of their tether.

Is the old gang of negaters lower in the plane of human intell=
igence than the greasers Stef was talking about?

A purely negative and cowardly opposition to Roosevelt has
been
a WASH OUT.

I am naturally foaming to know what if anything you discovered
in Paris or elsewhere/

I take it re/ the body of this letter: the first man to sound out
is Hamilton.[4]

At any rate do send on some sort of answer calculated to
restrain my nacherl foolishness.

                    cordially yrs.

Question in my mind whether ANYthing remains of republican
party
EXCEPT a few bankers; and the DuPont contingent. I mean
money ramp severed from manufacturers/ or manufacturers
simply
muddled to point of not knowing the difference.

What wd. be wrong with demand for COMPLETE
reorganization of Rep.
***

1. Edward Mandell House (1858-1938), an advisor to President Wilson, helped
draft the Versailles Treaty and covenant of the League of Nations ("House"). Cf.
Letter 18, n1.

2. Marrimer Stoddard Eccles (1890-1977) was an American economist. As governor of the Federal Reserve Board (1934-36), he was influential in pushing the Banking Act of 1935 through Congress. He was also chairman of the Board of governors of the Federal Reserve System (1936-51) ("Eccles"). Bernard M. Baruch (1870-1965) was an American financier, securities expert, and long-time government advisor ("Baruch").

3. Lincoln Steffens (1866-1939) was a noted American journalist and author ("Steffens").

4. Pound is referring to John David Miller Hamilton, the Republican political leader who became National Chairman of the party in 1937.

30. Pound to Tinkham

[5 November 1936]

Dear Mr Tinkham
             On the supposition that democratic fan mail
will be heavier than republican during the next few weeks

and/or that a deluge from me may amuse you amid the ruins
of Persepolis

AND without supposing that 100% of what I tap out will
have failed to occur to you ANYHOW,

surely NOW is the time for some one INSIDE the Repub/ lines
to INSIST on fact that the party committed suicide when it
put up a damn crook like Hoover and
                              succeeded in insulting
the whole people by getting that fat mugg into the
White House.
             The people had stood a good deal before that.

  Recovery on merely reactionary and negative lines is or
by right OUGHT to be impossible.

Either the old party died DEAD and stays dead and the
democs/ split into two real parties; god knows what
demarcation
            socialist nose=blowing/ doles ala England/

    heaven knows where it wd. divide.

OR the old skeleton takes up some clean and decent issue.

a way OUT; that is to say an ISSUE FROM the Nude eel
No question of changing just a FEW votes in 1940.

REEDUCATION; serious teaching of the REAL history of the
U.S.A.
           not the sixty years of suppression of the VITAL
              prolonging

facts.[1]

You are not going to oust Frankfurter with mere
non = intellectual
tosh; and few soft boiled lies that millions of people
now KNOW to be hoakum.

                national
That cold in the head is NOT is not going to be cured by
mere ignorance
                however many Liberty Bigs and Committees for
anti = nation get up and spend money.[2]

                                I note the Atlantic Digest
and the American Murkury are in SMALLER format.

John Danl (Webster) Miller Hamilton will have to assemble
at least a few {n} blokes who KNOW something.[3]

Obviously if the hired press hasn't cut any ice at the polls.

Taxes are unpopular/ but not unpopular enough.

Ham will have to learn difference between a tax and share.

Only way to beat Nude Eel ideology is to get a BETTER one,
                something with a drive/ not merely old fat.

Otherwise it will be Tugwell in 1940 and Frankfurter,
        Baruch; Morgenthstein; Isaacsohn, Ikevitch in the
Supreme Court.[4]

What about Hen. Ford; any way of boring a hole in HIS
skull.
                He had budged on a few inches/ got as far as
need of economic engineer, and had it printed in the Sat. Eve
Pustulence.[5]
                I cant get past his barricade of yes men and pubcty.
agents.
        I enc. spare copy of 8 questions, dated 1933. I emphasize the
date of printing; because they are not yet OUT of date.[6]
                                [no closing]

---

1. Pound felt that the views of Jackson and Van Buren regarding the
government's responsibility for money and credit had been suppressed since the
Civil War.

2. "Liberty Bigs" probably refers to the large financial interests that supported the Liberty League, a nonpartisan organization of conservatives who opposed the New Deal (Patterson 251-52).

3. J. D. M. Hamilton was the new Republican National Chairman. Cf. Letter 29, n4.

4. Pound's references to Isaacsohn and Ikevitch are unclear, although the latter may be his mutilation of the surname of Harold LeClaire Ickes (1874-1952), then Secretary of the Interior (1933-46) ("Ickes"). For note on Tugwell see Letter 12, n5; on Frankfurter, Letter 8, n13; on Baruch, Letter 29, n2; and on Morgenthstein (Morgenthau), Letter 8, n3.

5. Ford argued that both production and distribution would increase if industry were free to operate according to the production principles of high wages and low prices, rather than the opposite principles of "money men." "As prices come down to touch level after level of purchasing power," Ford maintained, "production goes up. And as a general and far-flung result, the standard of wealth and purchasing power of the whole community rises" (Crowther, "Our Job" 6). These principles would operate freely if left alone. "What we need is some financial engineers...free exchange has been so hampered [by government and finance] that production, distribution, and service have been made to look as though they have broken down" (Ford, quoted in Crowther, "Only Real Security" 6).

6. Cf. Letter 28, n3.

31. Pound to Tinkham

23 Nov
                XV [XIV] [1936] Hon G.H. Tinkham
Washington D.C.

Dear Mr. Tinkham.
                Enclosed item re/ Henry FORD. valuable.

These crank papers are the only way to get the news which
the hired press doesn't print.

My belief that F.D.R. will grab ALL the good issues/ and the
only effective opposition will be to get the BEST ones
BEFORE he does. and then HOLD 'em.

The boys in London like you. So you will get my note on
Landon, and if you have time; you will notice several
items between the lines of it.
                I mean; not only what I said
but what I was driving at.[1]

I suppose you are among the survivors// even if you weren't
        it wd. be worth doing a dying gladiator in the lame duck

and coming out for Congressional control of currency. So that
when the split comes you cd/ steer the right section.

Not enough data to interpret the Tugwell resignation.[2]
? a feint ??
                or a conscession to the usurers ? or ??

just better paid job for T//

                        I dont think T/ was venal.

anyhow the WORST diddlers are Morgenthau; Perkins and
Wallace.[3]

                ad interim
                                [no closing]

---

1. For citation on Pound's "note on Landon," see Letter 26, n3.

2. Tugwell had submitted his letter of resignation as head of the Resettlement Administration (RA) to Roosevelt on 17 November 1936, but the resignation was not effective until 31 December. His main reasons for resigning probably had to do with the RA's chances of getting appropriations. Since Congressional opinion considered him too progressive, the RA's chances were better if he resigned (Sternsher 322-25).

3. Frances Perkins (1882-1965) was U. S. Secretary of Labor (1933-45) ("Perkins"). Henry Agard Wallace (1888-1965) was U. S. Secretary of Agriculture (1933-40) and would be Vice President (1941-45) and Secretary of Commerce (1945-46) ("Wallace").

32. Tinkham to Pound

December 10, 1936

My dear Mr. Pound:

Upon my return from Europe on November 2, I went to Boston, where I remained until two weeks ago, when I came to Washington. Although I have not yet come to the end of the accumulation of work which I found upon my desk here, I am writing this letter so that you may know that your letter of November 23, with its enclosure, and your several earlier letters, including one which you addressed to me at London, have all reached me. Sincere thanks for them all, and for the literature which I have received under separate cover.

I am glad to know that "the boys in London like" me. I enjoyed very much meeting them. I regret I did not have the pleasure of seeing Major Douglas. "The boys" may have explained to you that he was out of town when I arrived and did not return until it was too late for me to meet him as finally suggested.

Enclosed is a press dispatch concerning my reelection which appeared in the principal Boston afternoon paper and which it occurred to me you might be interested to read. I understand it was copied over the country.

Believe me, with cordial regards and with the compliments of the Season,

Sincerely yours,
[signed] GEORGE HOLDEN TINKHAM

Ezra Pound, Esquire
via Marsala 12-5
Rapallo, Italy

33. Pound to Tinkham

Dec 24 [1936]

Hon. G./H/ Tinkham

My dear "Uncle George"

        I am sort of pinin' for a letter about

what it looks like from the inside. I dont hold it against [you]

(what you told me about Landon,[1] 'cause even the frigid T.S. Eliot
come back from Baastun all steamed up about the peril that
some blokes wd/ vote republican...)
                    //
The enclosed is fer yr/ hours of idleness. But considering
what the reps/ of the solid South get into the Congressional
Record (in the leave to print sections) it seems a shame not
to uplift 'em.

Print don't do it justice/ it must be sung in bar room
to get the full rhythmic richness.

                yrs devotedly

1. For note on Landon see Letter 12, n4.

34. Pound to Tinkham

[December 1936]

Hon/ G.H.T.

W.E. Woodward's

[Note: What is missing here is probably some reference to Woodward's book, *A New American History*.]

I shall review it in New Eng/ Weekly, but article wont appear for long time/ as other crisis stuff will precede it.[1]

I want to see if you think I exaggerate value of Woodward's moderation and horse sense.

Book OUGHT to be in all high schools.

most interestin'

(He is the Washington Image and Man; bloke)[2]

Hope you meet him.

WHAT is back of my mind is: YOU ought to be on nation's "mind"
   in press every day and all day till 1940.

Text book reform cd/ be presented in such ambiguous or vague terms that no one wd/ be alarmed. OBViously high schools shd/ NOT go on with text book obscurantism planned or slopped
during Grant's administration.
             II. I want you to get out WEST and let a few
          folks see you. OR spread the legend somehow;
             but I; from here, can't see better way than silent
                passage among the anonymous. (selected anons/)

Unless the character of the people in them paaats has completely
diliquesced I do NOT recommend such trip for most easterners
             I mean NOT as political move.

I think it wd. work on blokes like Hawk out in S. Cristobal N. Mex

(who is COMpletely anonymous).[3]

Have you any line on Col. Mack of S. Frisco.? runs a paper there,[4]

Any use my trying to write in Baaastun Travvelorr?

Re/ Text Bk/ reform. Woodward's book is a concrete and extant
      object. that CD/ be introduced.
                              Not mere matter of
vague wish.
           And his being a sort of democrat (not very) and
having been on Roper's[5] advisory whatever/
           might make him a strategic point.

when I say democrat; get it that he is ENTIRELY undazzled.

(as you wd. gather from the book anyhow.)

OH/ well AZ nooz (just come) Liveright[6] has sent on chq/ proving
that several copies of my Jefferson/Mussolini have actually been sold.
                [no closing]

1. The article appeared in *The New English Weekly* on 4 February 1937, and was reprinted on 11 February 1937.
2. This is the title of another Woodward book.
3. "Hawk" refers to Harold W. Hawk, a former student of Pound's at Wabash College, who had written a favorable review of *Jefferson and/or Mussolini* for "a Texas paper," probably the *El Paso Times* or the *Dallas News* (Hawk).
4. I can find no information on Colonel Mack.
5. For note on Roper see Letter 12, n5.
6. For note on Liveright see Letter 18, n4.

35. Pound to Tinkham

APPLY NOO YEAR. Jan. I [1937]

Dear "Uncle George"
        ABsent treatment you GOT to apply to me, but
possum treatment just aint necessary. I dont want to push you
(I see you ceding to pressure ANYhow!!) to indiscretion.

And if you dont want to SAY anything yet; I suggest you give
Senator Frazier a chance to work on you. Let him TRY to
convert you (and incidentally find out what he really knows).

I have had a sensible letter from him. He also suggests I try
working on the new governor of Dak/ for text book reform.[1]

NEXT; Is Amos Pinchot a serious character?[2] I have had
serious long letter from him. Good as far as it goes. But does
"NON partisan monetary authority" mean one that cares
a damn for the good of the country; or does it mean
Barney Baruch/ Vanderlip and a few more silent and
untrustworthy
non=partisans keeping things quietly wrong?[3]
        //
It having been PROVED damn well up to the next that
foreign business differs from INTERNAL business.

The NEXT fact to be burnt into public head is that SOME
GOODS
last longer than others.

        Difference in durability of tomatoes and bricks.
Demurrage charge.

NO NEED to use SAME tool (monetary tool) for all purposes.

A medium of exchange/ ANOTHER medium for savings.

STAMP SCRIP to correspond to PERISHABLE goods.
National bonds O.K. so long as you want to maintain rentier
class.
        They can STAY as a medium for saving.
Fixed gold certificates can properly be issued AGAINST actual
gold
        BUT not against hot air and banker's ink.

This PRACTICAL program will not satisfy doctrinaire theorists
>>> but it wd/ WORK.

I will elaborate if you wish.

The WEDGE to split the present swollen Roosevelt party COULD
be/ REFUSAL to accept restrictions of product BEFORE honest
monetary system is set up.
>>> EVERYTHING he does to keep OFF
MONEY is red herring.
>>> ArchBish
Re/ England/ That swine of Canterbury[4]/ spent summer on Morgan's
yacht.
>>> dont forget that. Since when Church has damped down
on economic justice.

All the filth in Baldwing buggery is {HHHHH} BANK
>>> Wiggin
>>> WIGRAM (alias {HHHHHHHHH}) and
the old stuffed anestheticia LORD {WIGAN,} who has been put
back to whisper sweet nothing into ear of Geo. VI
is or was director of MIDLAND BANK.

I am asking London for LIST of cabinet connections.

Hoare: of Hoare bank
Eden/ Beckett.
{Wigan} the palace pimp/ Midland. (permanent Lord in Waiting.[5]
WIGRAM
People who stood by Ed/ a handful of Fascists/ handful of
Soc/ Creditors/ a few communists and hyper = excitable people.

>>> AND the Catholic Times/ which had good front page/ to hell
with bankers' govt. (so good it was quoted entire in Doug's paper)[6]

At any rate for gorZAke RAG 'em about their red herrings

even if you dont want to start a definite program
prematurely.
[no closing]

1. Lynn J. Frazier (1874-1947), U. S. Senator from North Dakota (1922-40), was a member of the Committee on Banking and Currency ("Frazier"). On 9 April 1937 he was to submit a joint resolution "to restore to Congress the sole power to issue money and regulate the value thereof" (*Cong. Rec.* 9 Apr. 1937: 3313). When Pound says he wants Frazier to "work on" Tinkham, he is probably thinking of Frazier's ideas on money. The new governor of North Dakota was William Langer. At Frazier's suggestion, Pound had written Langer in December 1936. In his letter he offers his own *ABC of Economics* as a basis of economics textbooks in North Dakota schools (Pound, "To William Langer" 273).
2. Amos Richards Eno Pinchot (1873-1944) was an American lawyer and publicist ("Pinchot").
3. Frank Arthur Vanderlip (1864-1937), the assistant secretary of the treasury (1897-1901), was a banker, financial writer, and government advisor ("Vanderlip"). For note on Baruch see Letter 29, n2.
4. Cosmo Gordon Lang (1864-1945) was Archbishop of Canterbury (1929-42) ("Lang").
5. "Baldwing" is Stanley Baldwin (1867-1947), the British prime minister (1923-24; 1924-29; 1935-37) ("Baldwin"). Lord Wigram was Clive Wigram (1873-1960), a British courtier who had been private secretary and Keeper of the Privy Purse to George V and was currently Lord in Waiting and Extra Equery to George VI. For many years he was a director of the Midland Bank. ("Wigram, Clive"). The "buggery" probably refers to Pound's belief that Edward VIII, because of his social credit leanings and his desire to keep England out of the war, was forced to abdicate by the Baldwin government in collusion with financial interests (Materer 182-92; Davis, Earl 107). Samuel Hoare (1880-1959) was Viscount Templewood; he had been the British foreign secretary in 1935 ("Viscount Templewood Dead"). For notes on Eden and Beckett see Letter 12, n2.
6. "Doug's paper" was *Social Credit*, founded in 1934 by the Social Credit Secretariat, of which Major Douglas was the leader. The paper folded in 1939 (Finlay 139-42).

36. Pound to Tinkham

[January 1937]

Dear "Uncle George"
           Beaverbrook's Daily Express is referring to Ham
Lewis
and Borah as Shylock No. I and Shylock No. 2.[1]
           Someone ought to TELL England that the sending of
Runcy accompanied by Otto Ernst Niemeyer is enough cause
for severing ALL relation between the two countries[2]
           A little PEP in it.
                     London press seems to think the
kikes failed to pick Morgenthau's pocket...but who knows...

Some pilgrims at my father's yesterday were talkin about Lewis
as
the next president.
           Report dont say whether they meant "Ham"
or the Labour bloke...[3]
                 however it ought to be watched.
   Globe says they were to be on the stands at LAST, on
  of St Paul
               day Before yester/ but
gore knoze.[4]
           Leigh offering me tour in the U.S.[5] CD/ it be any
USE?? I suppose I shd. read poesy and "lecture" on
littercheer...IF etc// matter of timing whether it cd. [be]
used as feeler or to get things into the air .... At any rate
       my transport and expenses wd. be covered...
             BUT I shd/ want guidance
      before hand as to what was possible and/or advisable.

ALSO the choice of time very important. He suggests winter
of '37 or Fall of '38.
           Neither time any use to ME.
And other more interesting ways of using my TIME...
             there wd. have to be a REASON for
a tour, more than being looked at.
        Text book reform sproutin' mildly.

                ...Hope you are feelin' fit.

To the Hon. G.H.T.

1. Senators Lewis and Borah insisted on the repayment of the British war debt. In February 1937 Lewis was to submit a resolution prohibiting the U. S. from entering into any reciprocal trade treaty with any nation that refused to pay its war debt to the U. S. or that repudiated such debt (*Cong. Rec.* 19 Feb. 1937: 1398-99).

2. Walter Runciman, a British statesman, and Otto Ernst Niemeyer, a director of the Bank of England, both visited the U. S. in the latter third of January, 1937. Contrary to wide speculation that their visits were more than coincidental, probably tied to the agreement among Britain, France, and the U. S. on currency stabilization, the two men had separate agenda. Runciman, in what he claimed was a "private" visit, held talks with Roosevelt and Hull about U. S.-British trade. Although the currency issue was discussed, it was only in relation to trade. Niemeyer, claiming to represent neither the Bank of England nor the British government, met with the Foreign Bondholders' Association to discuss German and South American defaults. (Kuhn, "Trade Pact"; "Anglo-U. S. Treaty"; "Niemeyer Coming").

3. "Ham" refers to James Hamilton Lewis (1863-1939), the U. S. Senator from Illinois (1913-19, 1930-39) and former U. S. Representative from Washington (1897-99) ("James Hamilton Lewis"). The "Labour bloke" refers to the American labor leader, John L. Lewis.

4. *Globe*'s first issue came out two months later, in March.

5. William Colston Leigh (b. 1901) ran the leading lecture agency in the U. S., W. Colston Leigh, Inc. He specialized in contracting with returning American expatriates ("Leigh").

37. Pound to Tinkham

[January 1937]
Dear G.H.T.

       This letter is sent in order to make it possible
for you to say that a letter has reached you showing
american in favour of WAR with England at once UNLESS
state of things permitting the inclusion of Ernst Otto Niemeyer
       in a financial delegation to the U.S.
chief pimp to Monty Norman, is ENDED at once.[1]

(at mildest, one might suggest severance of diplomatic
relations...

       spose that, eva n [*sic*] that is impractical)
Inclusion of the dirty pimp IS useful as lighting up Paish
(most downy of bird, on whom so far as I know no
one has anything)
       and Runciman, "the invisible man".[2]

As usual NO real news gets thru. I hear Borah is O.K.
on the Brit. swindle.[3]
       //
State of England perhaps shown by FRONT Page two col.
headline
some farmer shot a FOX.
       (Last week whats his name V. Leech
was murdered/
       I think NOT a line. NOT A LINE
Ital/papers got it in connection with stabbing of Nevchine.[4]
       cheerio.

---

1. To say that Niemeyer was part of a "financial delegation to the U.S." was a misrepresentation of Niemeyer's visit (see Letter 36, n2). For note on Montagu Norman see Letter 8, n2.
2. Sir George Paisch (1867-1957) was a British economist, financier, and government advisor ("Paisch"). The epithet "the invisible man" may refer to Runciman's low profile, despite his highly influential role in the Baldwin cabinet.
3. The "British swindle" probably refers to Britain's default on its war debt to the U.S. (cf. Letter 36, n1).
4. I can find no information on either "V. Leech" or "Nevchine."

38. Pound to Tinkham

27 Feb [1937]

Dear UnKL George   Thanks very much
                          for the cuttings.
               That Washington Pust reminds me of the happy
rumour "Harding will listen" My impression of yr/friend Van
denberg was that he wouldn'T. Tho recently he was right about
something (forget what) when Bridges wasn't.[1]

Dewey[2] seems to have heard that a lot of govt. bonds are held
by banks. That is ONE tiny toddler's toddle toward light.

I wish you wd. do yr/parental duty by those young men.
They NEED a fatherly hand. and OUGHT to be grateful for the
chance of it.

Saw a wide blurb article re/Jo Martin.[3] all very complimentary.
I spose I ought to have seen him. BUT...and on other hand
the only good dutchman ever was Martin Van Buren.
I wish I cd/get a line on Bridges' economic comprehension (if
any)

I dont spose J. Lewis' plug for Wheeler wd/elect the latter.
The people might decently choose between Wheeler and Bridges
without being SURE of getting a slob.[4]

Didn't look to me as if the Wash. Post writer much WANTED
a republican president. Last year the dems/were all TOO damn
anxious to have Dewey nominated. Didn't smell right to me,
but then I am nearly a dago.

Also this son in law racket. With 200 years of history.
Hamilton (Alex) was I believe a snot, more I read, more it
appears so, but back of him was his pa/in/law. The snots
when they can't elect someone sure to sign on the dotted
plug for "YOUTH", which they think they {HH} can
bamboozle.[5]

               here's how.

If you have time for light reading, let me know, and I will send on my notes on J/Adams and the Chinese Emperors.[6]

1. Henry Styles Bridges (1898-1961) was governor of New Hampshire (1935-37) and then U.S. Senator from New Hampshire (1937-61) ("Bridges"). For note on Vandenberg see Letter 15, n1.
2. Thomas Edmund Dewey (1902-71), the New York politician, was to become governor (1942-54) and, in 1944 and 1948, the Republican Presidential nominee ("Dewey, Thomas Edmund").
3. Joseph William Martin, Jr. (1884-1968) was U.S. Representative from Massachusetts (1925-63). In 1936 he had been the Eastern chair of the Republican National Committee, and in 1940 he would be the National Chair ("Martin").
4. Burton Kendall Wheeler (1882-1975) was U.S. Senator from Montana (1923-47) ("Wheeler," *Biog. Dict.*). "J. Lewis" refers to the labor leader, John L. Lewis.
5. For note on the "son-in-law racket," see Letter 12, n2. Alexander Hamilton's father-in-law was Philip Schuyler, a general in the Continental Army and the foremost financial expert in the Continental Congress. Like Pound, General Schuyler bewailed the financial ignorance of the Congress, but from an opposite viewpoint; the general, along with his son-in-law, was a strong proponent of governmental ties with financiers (Miller 23, 52, 56).
6. These "notes" would eventually become the Chinese (52-61) and Adams (62-71) cantos, published by Faber on 28 January 1940 (Stock, *Life* 375).

39. Tinkham to Pound

March 31, 1937

My dear Ezra:

I am sorry I have not been able to write to you before. The work of my office has been unusually heavy recently, and following the Supreme Court proposal there descended upon me a deluge of protests.[1] In fact, I have never received so many letters on one issue since coming to Washington twenty-two years ago. With regard to the economic situation, my views have not changed fundamentally since we went off gold in April of 1933. In fact, what I predicted then is eventuating today. Basic commodity prices are rising. They are going to rise much higher. There are three reasons for this rise:

(1) During a depression basic commodity surpluses accumulate; as recovery begins, the accumulations are absorbed; there are increased biddings for basic commodities and prices rise. This is the normal and orthodox action and reaction in a depression and recovery; but in this country, two very artificial influences have been at work to precipitate the rise in commodity prices to great heights.

(2) Between 8 and 10 billions of what might be called "deficit" dollars have been issued and put into circulation. This has been done by a printing press bond method and has created great credit resources, with the same economic effect that would have been achieved had the Government printed the same amount of money in the form of what used to be known as "greenbacks". The purpose of so large an issue of money has always been to raise prices artificially, and the purpose has always been effected.

(3) There was an artificial reduction of the gold content of the dollar by 40 per cent, thus adding an enormous amount of gold. This action has stimulated the world production of gold to such an extent that 50 per cent more gold is being produced at present than was being produced in 1929. History over a period of 400 or 500 years shows that a large intrusion of gold has always powerfully increased basic commodity prices. The discovery of North and South America and of its gold, which went to Europe, finally increased commodity prices 300 to 400 per cent; the discovery of

gold in California in 1838 increased basic commodity prices, roughly, 50 per cent; and the discovery of The Rand in Alaska raised basic commodity prices about 50 per cent, - all very slowly, of course. In 1933 there was more gold in the possession of the *genus homo* than at any time in the history of the world, and since then there has been added the largest amount of gold ever added in a like period of time.

These three forces are increasing basic commodity prices inordinately and will continue to do so unless some action is taken. As any action taken would bring a panic, particularly in agricultural commodities, it is probable that no action will be taken by this wholly politically minded Administration which we now have in Washington.

Now, as to taxes. Not only is an immense amount of money being spent by the federal and local governments, but policies have been adopted which call for further large expenditures, so that taxes are bound to rise materially in time.

Labor costs are being pyramided, first, by increase of pay and secondly, by reduction of hours.

These three elements, basic commodity prices, taxes and labor costs, determine the cost of living, so the cost of living must rise, and this irresistibly, causing a fall in the purchasing power of national and international currencies. I say "international" currencies as well as national currencies because all the larger countries are pursuing about the same course.

From all this, as you can well see, will come political and social chaos. The denouement in the United States will come very probably between 1938 and 1941. I should rather be held to this span of years in this pre-diction, although quite tentatively I am picking 1939 as the year.

This, certainly, is a very unfavorable outlook and what can come out of it except a great disturbance and social and political dislocation I cannot see. Labor, encouraged by our wholly irresponsible president, is not only rampant, but defiant of law. All of these things could have been avoided by an administration which was conservative or by one which dealt with fundamental things and knew something about economic history and about deal-ing with the *genus homo* in the mass.

I am loath to write such a report, but I am com-pelled to do so by facts.

I hope all goes well with you.

It is now most uncertain when the Congress will adjourn. I do not know yet what I shall do this summer. I may fly the Pacific and spend several months in the Far East, or I may come to Europe.

I do not see war in Europe this year any more than I did when I left Rome last October. Of course, if France should collapse economically or politically it might come. I should be much interested in your views on this subject— whether or not you think there is a possibility of war in 1937 in Europe, also I should like to know what you think of the French situation, with which you must be quite familiar.[2]

With cordial regards, I remain

Sincerely yours,

[signed] GEORGE HOLDEN TINKHAM

Ezra Pound, Esquire
Via Marsala 12-5
Rapallo, Italy

1. Roosevelt had proposed that he should be empowered to appoint a new justice, up to a total of six, for each Supreme Court Justice who did not retire within six months after turning seventy years old. If his proposal had been approved, he would have been able to outflank the "nine old men" with six New Deal justices (Burns 293-94).
2. Pound responds in Letter 41.

40. Pound to Tinkham

II April [1937]

Dear "Uncle George"
                          I was glad to read of yr/ vote vs/ Federal
Reserve hoax. Curious to know whether you voted quietly or
with music.[1]
                          I am scared to death of making a noise too soon.
I think I wrote that GLOBE couldn't handle my note on the
League of Notions. At least not YET. They were pleased by my
note on Edward to=be Simpson.[2] BUT doubt if the magazine
got into
England.
                          And I dont know what the traffic will stand.
                                         //
Alberta news is good. Canadian news is good. Indian news is
also interesting.[3]

                          Spain keeps on USING guns.
Odon Por Says I shd/be cheered by economic development
here.
Old hoaxes failing slowly. De' Stefani gone to China.[4]
                          Anyhow, both Germany and Italy seem to begin to
see
that nations money shd/be based on national productivity.
Por in Revista del Lavoro claimed Hitler was out for National
Dividend.
                          The Fuhrer said "jeder Kontrahenten" ought to have
his part.
                          North Americ. Rev. dont like me, but the boys in the
VOU, Tokio, have been printing me every month for some time
in translations whereof I can make out just enough to see
                          what they are using.[5]

                          Let me know if ANY foreign information can be
useful.

                          yrs ever and keep AT 'em

1. Pound is referring to a Senate bill that would amend the Federal Reserve Act
to "extend the period during which direct obligations of the United States may
be used as collateral security for Federal Reserve Notes." He probably
considered it a "hoax" because it allowed the banks to profit at the government's

expense. In the words of Congressman Patman, who voted for the bill, but only because of its two-year limitation on the extension:

> It seems ridiculous...that the Government should issue a Bond drawing 3 percent interest, sell that bond to a Bank, then permit the Bank to deposit the Bond with the Federal Reserve Bank and get its face value in new money by paying the rediscount rate of 1 1/2 or 2 percent and continue to get 3 percent on the Bond. Then the Federal Reserve Bank by paying the cost of the printing...may get Federal Reserve notes – new money – on this bond without paying the Government a penny for the use of its credit, which guarantees the money, and will collect from the member bank the rediscount rate of 1 1/2 or 2 percent.

Tinkham voted against the bill "quietly," but it passed by a wide margin. (*Cong. Rec.* 24 Feb. 1937: 1563-64, 1571.)

2. For Pound's "note" see: "Abdication." *Globe* March 1927: 82-87 (Gallup, C1394). The magazine never published his piece on the "League of Notions."

3. "Alberta news" possibly refers to demands by "insurgents" in the Alberta legislature for more drastic monetary reform along social credit lines, and for the possible services of C. H. Douglas as advisor ("Alberta"). "Canada news" possibly refers to the legislative effort to control the munitions industry to outlaw war profiteering and to keep Canada free of entanglements that might lead to her involvement in war ("Canada Plans"; "Canada Studying"). Cf. reference to Spain "USING guns" in the next line. "Indian news" possibly refers to the deadlock between the British government and Mahatma Gandhi and the Indian Congress party over the new Indian Constitution, particularly in regard to the powers of provincial governors ("Britain is Seeking Talks").

4. For note on Odon Por see Letter 15, n8. Alberto De Stefani, the ex-finance minister, had become Italy's financial advisor to the Chinese government ("Italian Ex-Finance Chief"). The "economic development" that Pound is probably referring to here is the tendency, demonstrated in Italy, Germany, and China, toward greater national self-sufficiency and, as he perceived it, consequent economic justice for each citizen claimed by the Fascist state.

5. The VOU Club was a Tokyo-based group of Japanese poets who, under the leadership of Katue Kitasono, published *Vou*, a journal of contemporary poetry (Pound, *Kulchur* 137-39).

41. Pound to Tinkham

I2 April [1937]

Dear Uncle George
                    Yrs/ 3Ist. March to hand. And yr/ question
a fair teaser. Plain reply is: I know no more than a jack rabbit.
                    IM(damn)POSSIBLE to get any detailed news
out of
France.

I am convinced that Blum is NO damn good. Millionaire
Socialist fake.
                    ALMOST but not quite incredible that he
shd/be as
ignorant of economic fact as he pretends to be.
                    Anyhow. He is BAD. slush.. call him a jewish
Ramsay MacDonald.[1]

                    Daladier possibly a crank, but I think honest
and Laval practical.[2]

     One frog (who may be totally ignorant) told me I wasn't
utterly crazy to dream of a Laval Daladier hook up.

                    but it is all guessn and sky
writing

ALL I do see is CONTINUAL pressure to sell guns. This was
eased by a few sales in Abyssinia. The Spanish fake now permits
a limited sale in Spain,
                    without the unpleasantness of formal
war between European nations.[3]

India, Canada, Alberta, Italy, Hitler all getting wiser to London
(Jew and nonjew) Bank racket.

     I dont SEE why France shdn't just slump into general
sabotage
                    WITHOUT its starting a European war.

                    Swiss (german origin) bloke named Knitel to
lunch
                    will try to get inside his head, he has just
                    landed from Egypt on way to conferenze in Montreux

on Capitulations etc/[4] (in heaven knows what "capac/or incapacity
or merely trailing along.) I haven't made him out. But may get some Cairo gossip. IF I can keep from trying to explain the world to him.

THANKS for yr/two pages on American situation. No comment. I mean none from me. All that sequence of a cause and effect is perfectly clear and straight.
printing press
I shd/say the Bond rather accentuated the effect, or some of the effects, though mebbe makes 'em show a bit slower.

And tax on the actual money (Gesell stamp)[5] cd/be used to mitigate or do away with part or all of other taxes.
I shd/say (again mere guess) that Russia's internal disorder made it less likely she will attack others.

I am FOR the constructive efforts here and in Germany.

which take count of "genus homo" in its Italian and German segments.

I dont know whether my translation of Por's note on Milhaud plan
wd/interest you. As no editor wants to print it, I cd/ <u>lend</u> you the typescript.[6]

That is for international trade balance clearing bills that have a time limit/seems to me a sort of Guillo Gesellism, instead of gradual demurrage charge on the paper.

Supreme Court issue a damned red herring to keep public from
clear thinking about the power inherent in the right to issue money (alias right to issue enforceable claims against goods and services). Constitution much too honest a document to suit Barney Baruch.

I hear Admiral Dudley Pound (no relation) British Mediterranean fleet is in favour of
UNIVERSAL
currency.[7] I.E. a world money governed by a few London kikes.

Waaal THAT don't surprise me. Merely shows
that London city is misseducating the Navy.
                              to such lengths must
they go in pervertin' the simple minded sail/ors.

The Western segment of the U.S.A. at least might be kept awake
to the undesirability of the U.S. being governed by Mond and
Co.
        Imperial Chemicals and Niemeyer (Otto).[8]
                                        If this be
political mindedness on my part; make the best on't.

    Of course I shd/prefer you to come to Europe. But if
                      a look at
you go to Japan do have {in} the VOU club/ {HHHHHHHH}
co/
Kitasono Katue, I649 l'chome = magomachi, Omoriku Tokio.[9] IF
the Japs of their generation know as much about other
European
activities as the eight who have just sent me english
translations of their own stuff, do about contemporary poetry

there is a NEW Japan to consider.

                    A very nice and alert

and friendly Japan (so far as my friends are concerned) but at
any
rate not a negligible Japan. The Councillor of their Embassy in
Rome has been working for I7 years on a history of their poetry
IN
ENGLISH.
        These are the Japs who want friendly understanding. I
mean

COMPREHENSION...proper exchange cultural and
commercial.

No doubt there is interesting talk in Tokio.

                        Pleasanter prospect
than in Paris (ganz verJudet).

            Enough of this/I will try to collect
something more factual re/France... but apart from the

general desire of gunsellers to sell guns and financiers to finance the most rapidly consumable or destroyable products .... HELL! !

yrs.

1. Pound no doubt opposed Blum's monetary policies, which depended on British loans and served the private interests of gold sellers. In March 1937 Blum had arranged for "free imports of and commerce in gold and its purchase by the Bank of France without inquiry into the identity of the seller..." (Philip). James Ramsay MacDonald (1866-1937) was the first Labour Party prime minister (1924), head of the second Labour ministry (1929-31), and head of the coalition cabinet (1931-35); he was also Lord President of the Council in Stanley Baldwin's government (1935-37) ("MacDonald").

2. Pound had several reasons for approving of Daladier. Among them were his opposition to *La Comité des Forges* and large armaments expenditures, and his support of stamp scrip (Seldes 21-22; Pound, *Kulchur* 301). Pierre Laval (1883-1945) had been premier of France (1931-32, 1935-36), would become premier of Vichy France, and would be executed for treasonous collaboration after the war ("Laval").

3. While the Soviet Union had supplied arms to the Loyalists, Britain and France had not. Most of the influx of men and materiel had gone to the Nationalists and had come from Italy and Germany (Haines and Hoffman 415-17; Jackson, Gabriel 251-255). These facts make Pound's assertion about guns to Spain seem either misinformed or highly ironic, given his Fascist sympathies. He was probably getting his information from the Italian Fascist press. In the *Giornale d'Italia*, for example, a series of articles charged, in considerable detail, that both Russia and France had violated the non-intervention agreement by supplying both men and armaments (Cortesi). The "Spanish fake" may refer to either the Loyalist president, Manuel Azana; the prime minister, Largo Caballero; or the Loyalist government itself.

4. The Egyptian capitulation conference in Montreux would put an end to four-hundred-year-old treaties that granted special privileges to foreign nations in Egypt. The "capitulations" would be phased out by 1949. ("Powers Sign Pact"). Knitel is possibly the "Knittl" of Cantos 89 and 97 (but cf. Terrell).

5. The "Gesell stamp," or Schwungeld, was a form of paper currency to which the bearer had to periodically affix a postage stamp to keep it valid. The longer it was kept out of circulation, the less it was worth to the bearer. Therefore, it was a form of money that encouraged rapid circulation and discouraged hoarding (Laughlin 158).

6. Devised by professor Edgard Milhaud of Geneva University, the plan provided for the issuance of international purchase checks, payable in goods and services, in payment for imports. The checks, which were to be used within six months or a year, could be used to purchase commodities or services from any subscribing country. The checks were not convertible in gold, unless gold were bought as a commodity. The plan had wide approval and had been adopted by several countries, including France and Switzerland ("Urges Study"). For note on Por see Letter 15, n8. His "note," translated by Pound, was published a year later in

the July/September issue of the *British Union Quarterly* as "Systems of Compensation" (Gallup, C1409).

7. Sir Alfred Dudley Pound (1877-1943) was an admiral in the British Navy (1939-43) ("Pound, Sir Dudley").

8. Sir Alfred Moritz Mond (1868-1930), 1st Baron Melchett, was a British industrialist. He was a board member of Imperial Chemicals Industries, then the world's largest chemical company, closely associated with the British government and part of the war industries network (Brockway 247-252), which Pound despised. For note on Niemeyer see Letter 36, n2.

9. Kitasono Katue was the central figure in the VOU Club. He translated several of Pound's poems into Japanese. Cf. Letter 40, n5.

42. Pound to Tinkham

I4 April [1937]
P/S

Dear "U.G."
    Bloke from Cairo a mixed bag.[1] Lot of amusing
imitations of Ed/ viii, very drunk and very human/various
generals, Sauerwein (damn fool)[2] after interview with Hitler
                                                     only
ET/C// No clear line, and his opinions useful as indication of
opinions held in certain quarters.
                       He is believer in Thorez[3]

and thinks they will "hang" Blum (i.e. guillotine), and that
Rhoosia is goin forward.

Acc/ this bloke Various "authorities" admit they
underestimated
Mussolini (past tense) but don't seem to have learned not to
go on underestimating.
                an' thaZZATT

Specific datum today/
                   Italian papers carry with BERLIN dateline
a statement that French maconic powwow was for aiding
Spanish
reds to point of war
               and that Daladier held out against it
and was attacked for so doing.

                Friend of Daladier's wife told
me Daladier was not a macon.

                Either may be right.

My belief being that in any case Daladier has some sense
and enough to want to keep OUT of war.[4]

Card from Eng/says it was "one of the Dean's party" who
broadcast
the rot about Franco.

           I don't know that it matters.   But I will get it out
of Hewlett Johnson when he gets back to England.[5]

The only thing the pp/ re/ Daladier proves is that Italian press is willing to give <u>him a</u> friendly notice.

[no closing]

1. The "Bloke from Cairo" is the Knitel mentioned in Letter 41 (and n4).
2. Jules Sauerwein (b. 1880), a French journalist, was then editor of *Le Matin* and foreign editor of *Paris Soir* ("Sauerwein").
3. Maurice Thorez (1900-64), one of the founders of the Popular Front in 1934, was leader of the French Communist Party (1930-64) and a member of the Chamber of Deputies (1932-39) ("Thorez").
4. For notes on Daladier see Letter 16, n4, and Letter 41, n2.
5. The "Dean" refers to Hewlett Johnson, who, as Dean of Canterbury, had accepted an invitation from the Spanish government to investigate religious conditions in Spain. His "party" included Professor John MacMurray and Monica Whately, a well known Roman Catholic. Johnson was sympathetic to the Loyalist cause and critical of General Francisco Franco, especially for the bombings of Guernica and Durango ("Allows Mission to Spain"; "Dean of Canterbury": Johnson).

43.   Pound to Tinkham

5 May [1937]

Dear "Uncle George"   I.
WILL you or WUN'T you start drive for
"Congress shd/go on the AIR!"

???

(I can't put it straighter than that. Tho' I am ready for advice about timing.[1]

2.

GLOBE is under weigh. They tell me my Article on Eddie's abdication got a glad hand in EVERY review of the mag that they
recd//
What the Roman Empire will pull, gorrr noze.

3.

They sent back a piece by me damning the League of Notions and
saying the U.S.A. peepul ought to [be] eternally thankful to you and Borah (and the late etcs/) for keeping us out.[2]
As bizniz proposition Dunn has got to play with the majority at the last elections.

Mag/ "strictly non political".

Waaal; they printed a soft by Huddleston[3] on Spain, oh a soapy evasion of all things/
and Huddy in May number sez the
League is no bloody good.
which is so and wot of it.
good enough as far as it goes or dont go.

But no USE in particular.

LONG letter from Woodward (E.S.) of Vancouver Canada/not to
be confused with BILL W//[4]
saying what an son of an bitch is Aberhart.

I dont know whether you are interested in failure (not of Social Credit but of various ideas which I have held and HOLD false.)

&**************************

I.
Naturally there is NO credit without social ORDER.
2.
Monte dei Paschi/ 1624/ SOUND CREDIT/
                              based on abundance of nature
                    AND RESPONSIBILITY of the
whole people[5]

                    that is the SOUNDEST, of course MOST
of the

                    people cd/make a tolerable base.

3.
Doug/ dividends impossible without knowing at least roughly
that there IS a total profit to whole nation (or credit area)
for the period (year or whatever).

4.   Damn econ SECTS; instead of listening to valid criticism
OF

          other sects all start disagreeing BEFORE thinking.

5.   IGNORANCE of Italy, is no help.

          Rossoni's speech in Senate, printed in april La Stirpe,
is important.[6]

          Naturally WITH italian organization, amassi of grain
               and farm produce, they can DO things impossible
[with]

          unorganized commercial chaos.

               Someone ought to BRIEF the italian real news,
               you[7]

               Mebbe the Foreign Relations Committee
Wd/ pay for the necessary TIME.
                              I cd/supervise it, even if
not paid/
               Though no committee wd. have any faith in unpaid
help.
          not I I understand their natr//

Por and I cd/ oversee the briefing.[8]

                                    I cant take the TIME to DO
the job
        as it wd/leave me no time to earn anything by other
work.

        Unlikely {HHHH} Hull plus Phillips[9] wd/ gather or know bee
from
buzzard about such matters.

        Now DAMN it all; why dont you talk to Senator Bankhead
and find out what PUTT him off Gesell, AFTER he had hit
the high water mark of his career, and done the one spout that is
likely to putt him [on] historical map as a forerunner.[10]

{HHH} Neither Rossoni or Daladier are mere plain simps.

Daladier proposed Gesellism in Radical Congress 3 years ago.[11]
Rossoni in a few minutes made what amounts to more
constructive
            criticism than all the "disciples". I mean now
        I have had time to think over the implications and
        possibilities in Ros' VIEW.

                    NOTHING in contradiction to yr/remarks on
GOP.

    Do you see British Union Quarterly/my article in current
issue.
I asked 'em to send it to you/ BUT the brains have
left the office.
            {NewHLeagueHHpH} New Party being organized in
England,
        I dont know whether what has been LEFT in B.U.Q.
office like me or NOT.

At any rate they gave me head of list on the cover/ and
have printed my transition proposal.[12]
                    [no closing]

1. Tinkham never raised the broadcasting issue in Congress.
2. Cf. Letter 40, n2.
3. Sisley Huddleston (1883-1952) was a British journalist ("Huddleston").
4. E. S. Woodward, a friend of Aberhard, was an economist sympathetic to the
ideas of Silvio Gesell (Pound, "American Notes" 185; cf. Letter 41, n5).

Woodward's criticism of Aberhart may have concerned Aberhart's deficient understanding of economics. He had admitted that his social credit program had failed to deliver the promised dividends within the first 18 months of his administration. Moreover, the Alberta Supreme Court had overturned some of his social credit legislation. Major Douglas, like Pound, had little sympathy with Aberhart because he (Douglas) thought Aberhart misunderstood social credit (MacCormac). "Bill W." refers to William E. Woodward, the historian (cf. Letter 34, n1).

5. Monte dei Paschi refers to the Sienese Bank, established in 1624 (Edwards and Vasse 147).

6. For note on Rossoni see Letter 15, n6. His speech may have concerned the Fascist policy of "amassi," or storing of grain for use by the nation.

7. Tinkham did not act on Pound's suggestion to "BRIEF" the Congress about the "italian real news."

8. For note on Por see Letter 15, n8.

9. For note on Hull and Phillips see Letter 18, n2.

10. Cf. Letter 15, n9, and Letter 41, n5, on Bankhead and Gesell, respectively.

11. In his only major economic speech in the 1930s, Daladier spoke favorably of the Gesell-like experiment in Woergl, Austria – an experiment that was destined for oblivion after a brief success. Although Daladier used Woergl only as an example, it was seized upon, distorted, and used by his opponents to defeat his proposals. The Radical Congress was overwhelmingly against anything like a Gesellist monetary policy (Larmour 72, 270n).

12. The "brains" may refer to John Angus McNab (editor), John Beckett (Director of Publications), and William Joyce (Director of Propaganda), all of whom left the British Union of Fascists to form the National Socialist League (Cross 170-71). The article to which Pound refers is "Intellectual Money," published in the *British Union Quarterly*, April/June 1937 (Gallup, C1400).

44. Pound to Tinkham

I3 May [1937]

Dear "Uncle George"

Minor crisis in B.U.Q. head quarters as to whether you are to be provided with a free copy of last issue of their expensive Quarterly, containing me and Gen Fuller.

(The ex-edtr/ wd. have sent it. Their successor is applying to the Fuhrer for plenary powers).

The last three issues have been good.[1]
//
Chris. Hollis[2] "We aren't so Dumb", is worth seeing. General sanity on Europe, useful for Foreign Relations Committee unless they know more. Chapter on the U.S. unconvincing, but not fulsome (considering he has an administration job...in fact very calm..)
//
They tell me there is a bright INFANT m;c; named Voorhis from California...[3]

if he speaks to you, don't shoot the kid until you have looked at his teeth. There may be the makings of something there...

I can't guarantee anything, I report
direct remarks of his friends. He has graduated out of some ideas.
//
I dont spose Foreign Relations Com/has much to DO except NOT
have 'em.

Have they noted the Milhaud plan at all??
Intemperate Gesellism...but better than stagnation.[4]

ever

oh yes/a nuther young friend of mine met Stone[5] at
dinner a few weeks ago/letter just in/he SEZ EF
the rest of the Suprm/Judges are like THAT mebbe
Frankie better had chuck em ALL out and replace 'em by
kikes

1. The "last three issues" of the *British Union Quarterly*, formerly *Fascist Quarterly*, included a series of articles by Pound: "A Social Creditor Serves Notice." *Fascist Quarterly* 2 (1936): 492-99; "Demarcations." *BUQ* 1 (1936): 35-40; and "Intellectual Money." *BUQ* 1. (1936): 24-34 (Gallup, C1364, C1387, C1400). John Frederick Charles Fuller (1878-1966) was a British major-general and military analyst who belonged to the British Union of Fascists. Fuller wanted Fascism to create a society organized under political-military control (Skidelsky 319). The ex-editor was John Angus McNab (cf. Letter 43, n12).

2. For note on Hollis see Letter 15, n11.

3. Horace Jerry Voorhis (1901-84) was U. S. Representative from California (1937-47) ("Voorhis ").

4. Cf. Letter 41, n6.

5. Harlan Fiske Stone (1872-1946) was Associate Justice of the U. S. Supreme Court (1925-41) and Chief Justice (1941-46) ("Stone").

45. Pound to Tinkham

4 June [1937]

Dear "Uncle George"
New Yorker in Rome last week told me they
had got it all nicely sewed up to put in FARLEY in 1940.

If that don't arouse the ole fightin' sperrit
wot will!!!

One of Al Smiff's suite told the N.Y/er next day that it was
a dynasty, with Jimme R/ followin' poppah!![1]

Waaal!! what about Patman bill, chances??? I shd/like to
see a copy, to find out whether I think as highly of it
as English informant that it has chances.[2]
//
Rassagna I have been asked to write for
{Revista} Monetaria (about as
serious as there is.)

also for Volpe's [sic] very other magazine, that is the
Rivista di Politica Economica; office of Corporazioni or

at any rate Volp/ at the top of that pyramid.[3]

Which DONT mean they
are sure to print what I send 'em.

North American Rev/ after cabilling me in Siena last year, still
afraid to print Jefferson (as on P. II6, my Jeff Muss.)[4]

and SO on.

While being asked for Riv. Pol. Ec. I heard one on Volpe [sic]
that may amuse you/ someone observing him in early days in
the Balkans said:
That man is clever enough EVEN to
be
honest.

Matin reports some sort of scheme for
commercial credits.

I am asked for a note on these Chicago people

Empire Credit Foundation/ 24 million, of credits, so they say
or printed.

Anyhow, with Larkin's methods, etc. ideas are spreading.[5] I
mean
beyond theoretical circles.

Brit Union Quarterly SAYS they are sending you current issue.
(Macnab has left. dunno wot new edt. will be able to do
with it.)[6]
Mme Agresti regrets not having seen you.[7]

and thaZZatt.

ever

1. James Aloysius Farley (1898-1976) was Chair of the Democratic National
Committee (1932-40) and U. S. Postmaster General (1933-40) ("Farley"). Alfred
Emanuel Smith (1873-1944) was ex-governor of New York (1919-20; 1923-28)
and had been the Republican presidential nominee in 1928 ("Smith"). "Jimmie
R/" probably refers to James Roosevelt, the President's son; however, since he
was born in 1907, he would have been too young to run for the Presidency in
1940.
2. The Patman Bill, introduced by Wright Patman, U. S. Representative from
Texas (1928-76), provided for government ownership of 12 Federal Reserve
banks. Its intent was to remove bankers from the Federal Reserve Board and the
Open Markets Committee, thereby preventing private manipulation of money
and credit and, ultimately, "to stabilize and maintain a dollar of uniform
purchasing power" (*Cong. Rec.* 24 Jan. 1938: 1010; 25 May 1937: 5043; and 24
Nov. 1938: 362). Congressman Patman introduced similar bills throughout his
congressional career (*Congress and the Nation* 385).
3. Giuseppe Volpi (1877-1947), an Italian statesman and financier, was president
of the Italian Federation of Industry (1934-43). He had been a leader in the
Italian effort to intervene politically and economically in the Balkans in the
"early days" before World War I (De Grand, "Volpi").
4. In *Jefferson and/or Mussolini* Pound quotes Jefferson on his position against
interest-bearing currency (116-17); Pound uses the same reference in his article
on the Jefferson-Adams correspondence ("Jefferson-Adams" 320-21), which *The
North American Review* in fact *would* publish two months later in the August
issue (cf. Letter 24, n1).
5. For note on Larkin see Letter 8, n8.
6. Cf. Letter 43, n12, and Letter 44, n2.
7. Olivia Rossetti Agresti, a British journalist living in Rome, was a keen
observer of contemporary social and economic conditions. Although she did not
support Fascism, her writings nevertheless respected Fascism's constructive

efforts. Later she would translate Pound's essay, "What is Money For?," into Italian (Pearce and Schneidau 156).

46. Pound to Tinkham

6 June [1937]

Dear "Uncle George"
I am, naturally, pleased by bust London gold market.

McNair Wilson[1] will be all fireworks/at any rate the moment people begin to swap stuff OUTSIDE the field

governed by or affected in reference to the gold buggars

the metal's value is bound to come to its USE, out of

fashion for false teeth, and spectacle frames now made of fake tortoise shell.

Have you any line on the Empire Credit Foundation, of Chicago.
/// kikes onto something...

such az / trade balance clearings...

ever

1. For note on Robert McNair Wilson see Letter 12, n7.

47.   Tinkham to Pound

June 25, 1937

My dear Ezra:

Sincere thanks for "The British Union Quarterly", April-July, 1937. I was much interested in your article, "Intellectual Money".

Enclosed is a memorandum in relation to the Empire Credit Foundation about which you inquired. It would seem that they are not particularly reliable.

Enclosed also is a copy of the Patman bill to which you referred in your letter of June 4. No date has been set for its consideration by the Committee on Banking and Currency. Everything here is so confused it is impossible to say whether or not there is any chance of its passage during the present session. My guess is that there is not.[1]

At the moment I am up to my neck in work, and the weather has become quite intolerable.

I trust you keep well.

With cordial regards, I remain

Sincerely yours,
[signed] GEORGE HOLDEN TINKHAM

Ezra Pound, Esquire
Via Marsala 12-5
Rapallo, Italy

1. The Patman Bill was never passed. Hearings on the bill did not begin until 2 March 1938. The final hearing was 19 April 1938 (*Cumulative Index* 595).

48. Pound to Tinkham

10 July [1937]

Dear Uncle George
>Am sending you a spot of Confucius, sep/cov. Glad you cd/ read the Brit. Un. Quarterly article/ it was the third of a series, and I think the best. Wonder if the others ever reached you?[1]
>Wonder ALSO if any larger American diffusion of such discussion is possible?
>Thanks very much for copy of Patman bill/ and note on Chicago contraption (which might be O.K. IF .... last two letters being caps.)

//

>I wonder (recurring verb) whether you have YET got any line on why Sen. Bankhead got off Stamp Scrip?[2] souvenir enclosed.
>Mebbe if they were sent him in a Congress of U.S. envelope with interrogative 10th district stationary, it might elicit a spark or so.

Patman P/3 line 8/ "a generation hence" seems a bit ambitious and a bit unseasoned by historic perspective. AIM of bill seems otherwise O.K. and I suppose a bit of platonic exaggeration"
>etc/etc// as to ideal stability may. oh hell!!

>a bit more proportion wd/ be better.
>A purchasing power that is just, that doesnt

w***

violently,
that wd/adjust itself reasonably to available supplies
recognizing the GRADUAL cheapening of manufactured products
as process improves.
>That wd. imply a bit more judgment on part of the framer.[3]

The rest I have said already. Public (total pubk) shd/be able to buy available goods up to total amount WANTED for use, comfort, etc.

Idea of ABUNDANCE percolates slowly.

>cordially

1. The series of articles Pound wrote for the *British Union Quarterly* is listed in Letter 44, n1.
2. For note on Bankhead's stamp scrip proposal, see Letter 15, n9.
3. For note on the Patman Bill, see Letter 45, n2.

49. Tinkham to Pound

August 13, 1937

<u>Personal</u>

My dear Ezra:
        Mr. J. W. Dunn, Jr. has sent me four issues
of his new magazine GLOBE with advice that they were
sent to me "through the courtesy of Mr. Ezra Pound
of Rapallo, Italy".[1] Sincere thanks for your kind
thought of me in this connection. I shall read the
publication with interest.
        We now expect to adjourn about August 21.
It is my plan to leave at once for Bad Nauhein and to
remain there twenty-six days, then to go to Berlin,
Geneva, Vienna, Budapest, Prague, Paris and London,
and from London to Cape Town by boat, then to Johannesburg and back to London by air by way of Nairobi.
If it were not for my trip to Africa, I should plan
to spend two or three weeks in Rome, where there is
certainly much enchantment for me.
        I trust all goes well with you.
        With kindest regards, I remain
              Sincerely yours,
        [signed] GEORGE HOLDEN TINKHAM
Mr. Ezra Pound
Via Marsala 12-5
Rapallo, Italy

1. These were the first four issues of *Globe*. They included the following articles
by Pound: "Abdication." Mar. 1937: 82-87; "Europe--MCMXXXVI: Reflections
Written on the Eve of a New Era." May 1937: 106-10; "Revolution by Radio."
June 1937: 95-97; and "Net Result." July 1937: 101-104 (Gallup, C1394, C1407,
C1408, C1413).

50. Pound to Tinkham

22 Nov. [1937]

Dear Uncle George
                    What looks to me like a first rate scandal
SABOTAGE and bloody sabotage in the medical world. Not being a
specialist I am not claiming to KNOW.
                              BUT a bloke named
Tweddell has been curing pulminary tuberculosis CHEAP, for the
past 20 years/
                    inhalation of gypsom dust/ apparently workers
in the trade do NOT have tubercles/cattle that kick up
calceus dust do NOT have tubercles/
                              BUT (as might be expected)
Doc. F. Tweddell (Plandome N. J.) can NOT get any publicity.
                         Naturally IF his cure costs 2 dollars
for six months treatment/
                         AND the fancy blokes get I0 bucks
a shot for pneumothorax and theracoplasty they do NOT want
a poor man's treatment advertised.
                         THAT one can unnerstan/
BUT but damnd if I see why they shd/ get away with it.

Can you note it and VENTILATE/ especially if you are getting
round to investigating ENDOWments.[1]

Let me know if you want any data re/ events here.
                              I have been
spending my spare time on Confusius and Mencius and can read
more chinese than I cd/
                         bright lads in Tokio, writing good
poetry and translating me into Japanese.[2]

                    and so forth.
Hope you had a good trip, and regret not having made a
junction

---

1. Dr. Francis Tweddell (b. 1863) was a pediatrician who did research on tuberculosis ("Mrs. Francis Tweddell"). Tinkham did not "ventilate" the "bloody sabotage" in Congress.
2. Cf. "VOU Club," Letter 40, n5.

51. Tinkham to Pound

Personal

My dear Ezra:

I hope you will excuse my delay in replying to your letter of November 22, which I was delighted to receive. As I know you must appreciate, I have been under a great deal of pressure since returning to Washington for the special session.

The predominant opinion here is that we are having a minor depression. I am not going to make up my mind as to whether it is a minor or a major depression until March or April. A good deal will depend upon what the government does. I do not expect much that is sound, with the present Administration. All it will do very probably is to modify some of its most extreme measures. This would not suffice, with our whole economic structure heretofore eased upon decentralization of government and free economy.

My vacation in Europe was cut short by the calling of the extra session. I spent 26 days at Bad Nauheim, 8 days in Berlin, one day at Stuttgart, 8 days at Geneva, 9 days in Paris and 9 days in London. I had intended to go to Vienna for a week, to Budapest for 5 days, to Prague for 3 days, and then from Southampton to Cape Town by boat, to Johannesburg by air for a week, and then, by air, back to London, returning to the United States about December 31. I sailed from Southampton for home on the NORMANDIE November 3. A year ago I returned on the QUEEN MARY. The NORMANDIE makes the QUEEN MARY seem second or third class. It really is a most remarkable boat in nearly every particular. What surprised me was the quality. The boat is worth any one's taking a trip on it, or visiting it, no matter how travelled or critical he may be.

I think you are intellectually wise to divert your mind from the present state of affairs by turning to Confucius and Mencius. I envy you your enterprise.

Great historical events are occurring in the Far East and I am following them with much interest. I flew over the territory from the Trans-Siberian Railroad to Saigon, and over Nanking twice, and I can see it all now below me very plainly.

I trust you keep well. I know you keep busy.

With cordial regards and with the compliments of the Season, I remain

Sincerely yours,
[signed] GEORGE HOLDEN TINKHAM

Mr. Ezra Pound
Via Marsala 12-5
Rapallo, Italy

52. Tinkham to Pound

December 31, 1937

My dear Ezra:

It occurred to me that you might not see the enclosed page from the NEW YORK SUN of December 18.

I hope all goes well with you and that 1938 will bring you much happiness.

With cordial regards, I remain

Sincerely yours,

[signed] GEORGE HOLDEN TINKHAM

Mr. Ezra Pound
Via Marsala 12-5
Rapallo, Italy

53. Pound to Tinkham

[9 January 1938]

Dear Uncle George
                    Am early doing Mencius because he is
more explicit statement of where the Confucian ROOT (Ta
Hio)
sprouts in economics/against usury, against tax ramp.
                    I cant spread laterally so have to go DOWN into.
As for energy, I am trying to prod you onto a job that
needs a lot more. The voice of the people is there all right
in

> "He'll never die of hunger
> He'll never die of thirst
> Got one son with Dupont
> And another one with Hirst."

Time for you to cash in on yr/ record. I can't stand settin'
roun' with all that RECORD doing apparently nothing.
                    Might note that the only place I have succeeded in printing
yr/ name is in Mosley's "ACTION" with credit for keeping the
U.S. out of the bloody League of Nations.[1]
                    Took a year and a half to get that paragraph of Jefferson's
into North American Review.[2] Undt dtenn I findts in th' office
Mister AUSSlander!! ZION!! ZION!![3]
                    Ef you dont give 'em Texas QUICK they'll
take every state in the union.

Waaal; by geez; I'd like to see you stand on that
ONE paragraph of Jefferson's, even if it were only like
Van Buren standing on the anti=slavery ticket. It wd/ make
notch in the stick.

                    yrs ever

---

1. *Action* was originally the organ of Oswald Mosley's New Party, founded in 1930. It was later revived, in 1936, as the organ of Mosley's British Union of Fascists (Cross 44-52, 141).
2. The "paragraph of Jefferson's" appeared in *The North American Review* in August 1937 (cf. Letter 24, n1, and Letter 45, n4).
3. Joseph Auslander (1897-1965), an American poet noted for his romantic rhetoric and treatment of classical and biblical themes ("Auslander"), was poetry editor for the *North American Review* (1936-39). He was outspoken in his

sympathy for Jews and other victims of Nazism. Cf. "O Jerusalem, Jerusalem!" (Auslander, "Words").

54. Pound to Tinkham

I2 Jan [1938]

Dear Uncle George
     Mixed bag of notes.
I. Canadian usurers probably have created a record. Refusing
to allow an expert advisor, invited by Aberhart to Alberta
to stay in Canada.[1] There is NO limit to bank tyranny but
it sometimes gets picturesque.
   I enc. two cuttings. Ford is gradually getting pried into
place.[2]

  Science 2. Cultural front //
    Tweddell's cure for tuberculosis. Good popular stuff.
Cows stir up calcium dust. Gypsum workers breathe it. Neither
have tuberculosis. British doctors refuse to regard these facts
as data for science.
      Dr. F. Tweddell, Plandome N. J.[3]

3. cultural front/ microphotography for musicology and oriental
    studies.
      Milan Paper now in Fourth year/ Lingua
Estere/am
trying to start 'em on a THREE language system.
(esperanto, Occidental etc/ wont succeed. BUT a three
language
system/ a latin idiom, say Italian/
    Chinese ideogram/ taught by bilingual texts/
Kitasono[4] in Tokio on this//

    English, as only possible medium or middle ground
between STATES of mind represented by inflected language
   and ideogram, where one word can be all parts of speech.

    enough for this a/m/

         com'mon over for a little
music.

1. Alberta prime minister William Aberhart, having failed to make good on his
promise to give each citizen a monthly dividend of $25, and having recognized
that his version of social credit would not materialize, was compelled to ask
Major C. H. Douglas (cf. Letter 8, n7) for assistance. Although Douglas, through

his representatives, provided social credit legislation intended to salvage Aberhart's program, the legislation was blocked by the Canadian government (Elliott).

2. Pound may be referring to the possibility of a Ford presidency in 1940. There had been talk in 1937 of his running on a third-party ticket, but he had denied such intentions ("New Party Invites").

3. For note on Tweddell see Letter 50, n1.

4. For note on Kitasono see Letter 40, n5.

55.   Pound to Tinkham

I6 Jan [1938]

Dear Uncle GEORGE
A few days [ago] I got notice that I had been
eel = ected a MEMBER...and judging from the list of antecedent
members I reckon it must be the membrum virile which was
certainly lacking....OF the American InstitOOT of Art (or Aht)
and Letters.
Has this institution any official standing? Can a
segment of the Tinkham staff be detached for ten minutes to
find out?
As Brooks Adams, Henry Adams and Hen James belonged
to
it, I can't be too contemptuous of it. The intention is manifestly
honorific, but I can't make out (from the printed matter) that
it has DONE a damn thing during the 40 years of its existence.
The Sec. has carefully arranged that the LETTER
to be read at the annual etc/on Jan I8 can NOT get there in
time. I mean they ask me for a letter. Waaaal ole Hen James
told me what happened when they asked HIM for a letter and
GOT
it.... so that all gravy and bacon.
I have naturally taken ACTION. I mean within
24 hours I exercised several privileges, such as suggesting that
the way to elevate the status of the BODY wd/ be to get in
a few of the better writers (sent a list of ten or a dozen).
The membership is limited to 250 including
MEWsicians and PAINTERS (the hand not house variety).

I haven't counted the members, but say there are 80 writers
in the show// they COULD be mobilized and are NOT hired by
any one gang of newspaper owners (at least NOT at the
moment).
That is a potential force that could be used. I shall nat =
urally start driving for decent reprint of the gist of John Adams,
Jeff/Van Buren etc.[1]

Adams [handwritten emendation]
Saml H. {Hopkins} (not in the inst.) has been tackled
on this by old Bib Ibbotson (who is or was on some national
library committee).[2] Sam is FOR, but busy.

It strikes me that any public man OUTSIDE the

institute COULD make himself felt by public notice of it. If you get me.[3]

I dont know how feasible it is. The Inst. is ALL the Inst. there is. A question as to whether it is official, cd/ be perfectly noncommittal. But the members shd/in a civilized country
be interested by hearing such a question asked.

They sent an, god hellup us "insignia".
I didn't know these existed in the U.S. I suppose it has about the status of the button of the Royal Order of Buffaloes??? Nevertheless it is supposed to indicate distinguished serVices to aht or lettahs. It would be official in France, for example (where the kikes come from Bonnet's noses LONGER than Blum's.)[4]

At any rate if this starts a train of thought, do INDICATE
[No closing]

1. One month later, on 14 February 1938, Pound did in fact press for the publication of this material. In a letter to the secretary of the National Institute of Art and Letters, Henry Seidel Canby, he wrote:

> A job, and I think the first job for a serious Institute is the publication in convenient form of the thought of John Adams, Jefferson and Van Buren.
> That kind of thing is particularly the sort of thing an Institute could and should do. (quoted in Stock, *Life* 352)

2. Samuel Hopkins Adams (1871-1958) was an American journalist and author who wrote fictional and historical accounts of the Harding Administration and a biography of Daniel Webster ("Adams"). Joseph Darling ("Bib") Ibbotson (1869-1952) was librarian and professor of English literature, Anglo-Saxon, and Hebrew at Hamilton College, Pound's *alma mater*. He was Pound's teacher and long-time correspondent (1935-52) (Pilkington 4).
3. If Pound was hinting that Tinkham should take up the issue in Congress, the Congressman ignored the hint.
4. Georges-Etienne Bonnet (1889-1973) was French foreign minister under Daladier (1938-40) ("Bonnet"). For note on Blum see Letter 8, n5.

56. Pound to Tinkham

23 J Feb [1938]

Dear Uncle George
            Well, Eden is OUT.[1] And I am wondering if
there is or oughtn't to be a Scotch proverb
                "an' th' devil's welcome to him if
he likes flies in his parritch."

I have at last thought of something useful. Get me over
    to Heaavud or Yale to give a few lectures on Confucius
and Mencius.
            With the light of two thousand years of Chinese
history, there wd be NO NEED to allude to the present
administration or indeed to anything later than the
founding of the Ming dynasty.
            Naturally you wd/ not appear. Some respectable
and non political old gentleman from Back Bay wd/ insert
the bomb. Eliot, confound him, is holding over my Mencius
till June (good editing as Faber ought to have time to
bring out my Guide, with the note on the Analects before
    the Mencius appears,[2] AND naturally I can't let T.S.E. in
    on any ulterior reasons for wanting the essay printed sooner.
His firm's interest, such as it is etc.etc.
            waaaal good luck and a pleasant spring time
                        [No closing]

1. For note on Eden see Letter 12, n2.
2. Pound's "Mang Tsze (The Ethics of Mencius)" would appear in the July 1938
issue of *The Criterion*. His *Guide to Kulchur* came out shortly thereafter, on July
21. It had been ready for publication in June, but was held back for last-minute
editing of 15 pages that Faber had considered "possibly libellous." Pound's digest
of Confucius' *Analects*, previously published in English as *Confucius, Digest of
the Analects* in June 1937 by Scheiwiller, was included in *Guide* as chapter one
(Stock, *Life* 346, 354). Eliot ("T. S.E.") was a board member and editor at Faber
and Faber and editor of *The Criterion*.

57. Pound to Tinkham

I5 April [1938]

Dear Uncle George
        The RIGHT thing said about the Goldsborough Bill
spells I940 (nineteen forty).
        Say it with both barrels.[1]

The swine and liars dont seem to be having it their
own way with the committee/ esp/ Ford M/C/ seems to
have made a fairly pertinent enquiry to that stiff from the
N.Y. beanery.[2]

[No closing]

1. The Goldsborough Bill, proposed by Representative T. Alan Goldsborough of Maryland, was intended "to provide a national monetary policy which [would] have a definite relationship to the requirements of domestic industry and trade under the conditions imposed by [the nation's] power economy, which [would] increase production and consumption to the limit of the country's power to produce ...." It would control commodity prices through the issue of $10 billion in interbank currency as a revolving fund for the maintenance of buying power among retail consumers, who would be granted 15% of credit on each purchase, which could be used to buy other goods (*Cong. Rec.* 8 June 1937: 5438; "Angus Would Set Up $10,000,000,000 Fund"; "Backs Retail Discount").
2. Pound often referred to universities as "beaneries." The reference in this case is probably to Nicholas Murray Butler, who was president of Columbia University at the time, as well as president of the Carnegie Endowment (cf. Letter 1, n2). "Ford M/C/" refers to Thomas Francis Ford (1873-1958), a foreign trade expert who was U.S. Representative from California (1933-45) and member of the Banking and Currency Committee and the Foreign Affairs Committee ("Ford, Thomas Francis").

58. Tinkham to Pound

April 19, 1938

My dear Mr. Pound:

I regret exceedingly that there has been so long a delay in replying to your inquiry concerning the National Institute of Arts and Letters contained in one of your communications to Congressman Tinkham.

The National Institute of Arts and Letters was founded in 1898 by the American Social Science Association. Its present President is Walter Damrosch. The following have also served as President:

Charles Dudley Warner	Augustus Thomas
William Dean Howells	Cass Gilbert
Edmund Clarence Stedman	Robert Grant
William Milligan Sloane	Maurice Francis Egan
Henry van Dyke	John C. Van Dyke
John White Alexander	Arthur Twining Hadley
Brander Matthews	William Lyon Phelps
Edwin Howland Blashfield	Wilbur L. Cross

Mr. Tinkham seems to think that there is no organization in the country of its kind with a higher standing.

With all good wishes, I am

very truly yours,
[signed] G. C. Hamelin
Secretary to Mr. Tinkham

59. Pound to Tinkham

<u>PERSONAL</u>

I0 May [1938]

Dear Uncle George
          Waaaaal, we live to learn/ and/or as
Cato said.[1]
      A bright young lad of the younger Mellon set[2] has just been
telling me all about America. He sez in them
circles things are etc//
          And you can't be president because
you are "an excentric", you "wear a beard and never take a
bath. No man with a beard can be president.["]
            They might be polite
to you because you have a bank account, but you are not ONE
of them.
      (seems to me a damn good thing, but still)
Also Bro/ Goldsborough is an excentric. He goes round and
actually
speaks to the farmers.[3]

I suggested the election returns might cause thought even in
the heights of capitalist idiocracy/but this didn't seem to
convey anything. "They" had heard of young Lodge,[4] but you
just got elected somehow.

AS NO American ever seems to know anything about any other
American, I now set down a few points visible from here.

I. These California dated money people SAY they are having
whoopie.
But damn 'em they have gone off on DOLE (not dividend).[5]

Now to repeat/ DIVIDEND a la Donglas is a divide up of
the EARNINGS of dead men who can't eat 'em.
WORK still being done by EDISON's mind, or by Carleton's
{work}

                        inventions[6]
on wheat bending etc/
It is ETHICAL/
DOLE rots/ it is canker/ get details of
the way it IS absolutely rotting hell out of English working

class/ or now non=working class. human deterioration
APPALLING.
I am not going by newspaper, but by direct testimony brought
me
here by direct observer.
                          //
Young Lafollette/ according to program printed in London has
AT
LAST and for the first time so far as I have seen GOT hold
of something sound.[7]
                         Damn it all I wish he wd/back you
and then follow you.

I suppose the Goldsborough hearing in committee has been
timed
so as to keep bill OFF the floor of the House??[8]
                        //
May amuse you, in this connection to know that Dad got out
some old obit of my grandfather, last sunday. Milwaukee
Journal; I think it was. Said the Pound rule, at least in 1914
was still used to prevent the speaker from shutting out
discussion of any measure he personally disliked.

                T.C.P.[9] having been lieut/governor in Wisconsin
KNEW damn well what speaker could do; under old procedure.
I believe he staved off a fool bill single handed with
purely imaginary mover and seconder, on one occasion. And
when
        they had got him out of the state into Washington/ they
bitched
their river control and ultimately lost millions in
flood damage.

                All this Wisconsin nucleus dates I think from
mugwumps and first election of Cleveland/

Oh yes; other item is these Mellonites look to Kennedy...[10]

Lewis[11] meaning sheer class war/ I.E/ an out of date conflict
leading nowhere and wasting 25 years of human time for
the U.S.
        gawdDamnit.

                        devotedly yrs

1. Pound is probably referring to Marcus Porcius Cato, the elder (234-149 B.C.), an austere Roman statesman, orator, and writer, known also as Cato the Censor ("Cato").

2. The "younger Mellon set" included Andrew Mellon's nephew, Richard King Mellon, who was president of Mellon National Bank, and Andrew Mellon's son, Paul Mellon (Carroll). The Mellon family interests included coal, iron, and international banking. Andrew Mellon himself had been U.S. Secretary of the Treasury (1921-32) and ambassador to Great Britain (1932-33) ("Mellon").

3. Thomas Alan Goldsborough (1877-1951) was U. S. Representative from Maryland (1921-39) ("Goldsborough"). Cf. Letter 57, n1.

4. Henry Cabot Lodge, Jr. (1902-85) had just been elected U. S. Representative from Massachusetts (1937-44; 1947-53).

5. The "dated money people" in California were advocating a plan whereby "every senior citizen of California who is fifty years of age or over who has retired or will retire from active business or employment for compensation" would receive $30 a week for life. The money would be paid in stamp scrip. The idea was to increase purchasing power and open up jobs for citizens under fifty (Canterbury 408-10).

6. Mark Alfred Carleton (1866-1925) was an American plant pathologist and botanist whose importation of foreign grains established the durum wheat industry ("Carleton").

7. Robert Marion LaFollette, Jr. (1895-1953) was U. S. Senator from Wisconsin (1925-47) ("LaFollette").

8. The hearings on the Goldsborough Bill had begun on 8 July 1937 and continued intermittantly through 10 March 1938 (*Cumulative Index* 595).

9. Thaddeus Coleman Pound (1833-1914), Pound's grandfather, had been lieutenant governor of Wisconsin (1870-71) and U. S. Representative from Wisconsin (1877-83) ("Pound, Thaddeus Coleman"). As president of Union Lumber Company of Chippewa Falls, he issued stamp scrip redeemable in company commodities (Laughlin 151).

10. The reference is to Joseph Patrick Kennedy (1888-1969), the American millionaire, who had been chairman of the Securities and Exchange Commission (1934-35) and was currently ambassador to Great Britain (1937-40) ("Kennedy").

11. The reference is to John L. Lewis, the labor leader.

60. Pound to Tinkham

26 May [1938]

Note//
    in case it has missed you
SCHACHT during the Roman love feats has come out VERY
clear
for monetary ideas that I was pestering you with in Venice.

Ribbentrop apparently started letting parts of the cat out
last year at Leipzig fair/ Hitler this spring/ and now
Hjalmar H. Greely Schacht to all intents using my definitions
(naturally in blissful ignorance of the honour),[1] but still
it OUGHT to finish off the Salters/Keyneses/Guggenheim
Gregories and Sprague's harvard cronies.[2]

devotedly yrs

To the Hon. G.H.T. Tinkham

1. Schacht (see Letter 8, n8), Hitler, and German foreign minister (1938-45) Joachim von Ribbentrop (1893-1946) ("Ribbentrop") had voiced economic ideas that were "Poundian" in that they were based on national self-sufficiency. These ideas included a version of stamp scrip called "delivery drafts" that were not to exceed available funds and were to be redeemed within six months, a currency backed up by German industry instead of gold, and a general emphasis on German industry and internal trade as the economic base (Tolischus, "Germany's 'Right' "; Tolischus, "Reich is Shifting"; "Fuhrer at German Motor Show"; and "Nazi Election Crusade").
2. While "Guggenheim" refers to the family of American capitalists, industrialists, and philanthropists, the other names refer to influential economists. "Gregory" is probably Theodore Emanual Guggenheim (Gregg) Gregory, a British economist and author of *Gold, Unemployment and Capitalism* (1933) (Pearce and Schneidau 136; Edwards and Vasse). For notes on Salter, Keynes, and Sprague, see Letter 4, n3, and Letter 15, n4 and n8.

61. Tinkham to Pound

July 27, 1938

My dear Mr. Pound:

   Congressman Tinkham is now abroad for several months. Upon his return there will be placed before him the copy of LA VITTORIA received from you this morning, for which please accept my thanks on his behalf.

   Sincerely yours,

   [signed] G. C. Hamelin

   Secretary to Mr. Tinkham

Mr. Ezra Pound
Via Marsala 12-5
Rapallo, Italy

From Mr. Tinkham's <u>Itinerary</u>:

August 2-6, Geneva
" 8-14, Vienna
" 16-23, Budapest
" 25-29, Prague
Sept. 1-7, Paris
" 8-23, SS CARNOVAN
CASTLE to Cape Town
" 24-28, Cape Town
Oct. 1-8, Johannesburg
" 10-17, in air to London
" 19-24, London
Nov. 1 arrive in New York

62. Tinkham to Pound

August 5, 1938

Mr. Ezra Pound
Via Marsala 12-5
Rapallo, Italy

My dear Mr. Pound:

This week, in the absence of Congressman Tinkham, there have been received from London (1) a copy of the July September, 1938 issue of PURPOSE and (2) a copy of your book,
"Guide to Kulchur". Both publications are being placed upon the Congressman's desk for his attention when he returns from abroad. I know he will appreciate your kind thought of him .

Very truly yours,
[signed] G. C. Hamelin
Secretary to Mr. Tinkham

63. Pound to Tinkham

I0 Dec [1938]

Dear Uncle George
                Roosevelt "for the capitalist system"
???? meaning the present unconstitutional mess and abrogation
by govt. of the sovereignty vested in it??

Hell! why not a constitutional party?

  Yr/ friend Schacht after having come clean with an
honest definition of money, has now flopped, and shows
himself to be no more trustworthy than Sieff; Norman or any
damn jew.[1]

When next in England I hope you will meet General Fuller[2]
                                    (J.F.C.)
Have just spent six weeks in that muggy island.
                cordially yrs

1. Schacht had proclaimed that necessity had forced Germany to abandon certain
economic policies in favor of external trade and credit expansion (Tolischus,
"Schacht Upholds Nazi Trade Policy"). For notes on Sieff and Norman, see
Letter 18, n5, and Letter 8, n2.
2. For note on Fuller see Letter 44, n1.

64. Pound to Tinkham

[21 Dec 1938]

Dear Uncle George
        Enclosure shows that European NEWS sense is progressing/ pity we cant have a bit of similar NEWS from Nee Jew York.
        A who's who of British Parliament is being serialized showing what which M/Ps are directors of/ also Milfordhaven as director of Marks and Spenser.[1]
                                        AND so forth.

                        in the Spring
Hope if I git to Washntn you wont be skylarking off on a Easter vacation or something frivolous.
                                        [no closing]

1. Sir George Mountbatten, 2nd marquess of Milford Haven, second cousin to George V, and Queen Victoria's great-grandson, was a prominent businessman ("George V's Cousin"). Marks and Spenser Ltd. is a British department store chain, established in 1926 by Lord Marks, who was Israel Moses Sieff's brother-in-law ("Marks & Spenser Ltd."; "Lady Sieff Dies"). Cf. Letter 18, n5.

65. Pound to Tinkham

I3 Jan [1939]

Dear Uncle George
                I enclose a carbon that needs no
explanation.
                The Skoda drive for war last year STINKS/[1] I spent
some
weeks in England. Bloke who had been
in their secret services, with references to the "CITY"
said he cd/ buy any of the big politicians EXCEPT
Chamberlain.[2]
                He also had the dope on ALL the communist
leaders, some of the lower men honest, but the rest definitely
paid by Russia for military espionage.
                The devilment in the U.S. I keep on repeating is
in their efficient PUBLISHING propaganda.
                Has taken me years to get John Adams' works, whereas
Stalin, Lenin, Trotsk, Marx on sale at I0 cents, and 25 cents,
in editions of I00,000/
                Sweepings of european ghettos come to
attack constitution without bothering to know what is in it.
Said admirable document BETRAYED by every god damned
stinking
administration since Andy Johnson.
                Waaaal; ef you and Bill Rearer and young Jerry cant
turn out Rosevfeld, Baruch and Morgenstein Ltd/ I shall
register delusion.[3]
                I see young Jerry (Voorhis) had sense enough to
start a speech by quotin' J. Adams/ but do educate him NOT
to quote or read Keynes. Schacht as I told you had
used a decent sentence re/ natr ov MONEY.[4]
                [No closing]

---

1. Skoda was a Czechoslovakian industrial complex that was one of the world's largest producers of munitions and armaments during both world wars ("Skoda Works").
2. Arthur Neville Chamberlain (1869-1940) was British prime minister (1937-40). He sought peace through negotiations and appeasement with Mussolini and Hitler while Britain rearmed ("Chamberlain").
3. I have not been able to trace "Bill Rearer." "Young Jerry" refers to Jerry Voorhis, U. S. Representative from California (see Letter 44, n3). "Rosevfeld" and "Morgenstein" are Pound's Hebraized spellings of "Roosevelt" and "Morgenthau."

4. Cf. Letter 60, n1, but also Letter 63, n1.

66. Tinkham to Pound

January 14, 1939

<u>Personal</u>

My dear Ezra:

Sincere thanks for your letters of December
10 and 21. I am delighted to know that you
may be in Washington in the Spring. Please let me
hear from you the moment you arrive.

You may be interested to know the semi-civilized
and barbarous places with which I had geographic contact
during last Summer and Fall: Washington, New York, Bremen,
Bad Nauheim, Frankfort, Berlin, Geneva, Vienna, Budapest,
Prague, Madeira, Cape Town, Johannesburg, Pretoria,
Durban, Mozambique, Mombasa, Nairobi, Kisumu, Khartoum,
Alexandria, Rome, London - 28,000 miles, about 13,000
by air.

With cordial regards and best wishes for 1939,
I remain

Sincerely yours,
[signed] GEORGE HOLDEN TINKHAM

Mr. Ezra Pound
Via Marsala 12-5
Rapallo, Italy

67.   Pound to Tinkham

20 Jan [1939]

Dear Uncle George
                    Considering the extent whereto the Nation has
been bitched by dumping swill into it, since 1866, not only
swill of Europe, but the slop of descendents of tartars, so
low in the human scale that even a conversion to Judaism
means a cultural advance/
                    AND considering bolchevism AND
I suppose Frankie being left with only yitts and yes = men,
the constructors, or good = intenders like Warren and Tugwell
having died or gone/[1]
                    wdn't it be in order to refuse
admission (or at any rate nationalization) to anyone who
couldn't pass a stiff exam. in the U.S. Constitution, really
show understanding of it, and THEN swear to support it.

Have you either heard or have read Voorhis whoop, of June 6th
1938.
          not to be taken verbatim. But the opening quotation
is good.[2]
//
Realize what it signifies that it took me seven years to
                    an edition
get hold of John Adams writings ....
more one digs into 'em the more a MIRACLE one finds
our start. 1760 to 1860/ or at any rate the revolution
itself. Knowledge of same being snowed under 4th July
rhetoric, as fluid in {our your} time of our youth.

                              ever

      I haven't copy of naturalization law as
   it now stands/ believe there IS
a vague something about an oath/ but
not much prerequisite UNDERSTANDING.

1. For note on Warren see Letter 15, n8; for note on Tugwell see Letter 12, n5.
2. Cf. Letter 65, n4.

68. Pound to Tinkham

20 Jan [1939]

Dear U/G
    sorry to be so frequent, but paragraph in Eclaireur de Nice sets me off. It says Rosenvelt wants you to PROLONG his financial powers. DAMN it do YOU never READ the constitution
Of course Baruch and CO/ don't give a damn about that document.

ARE you still on the Committee for "affairs concerning the Pres"?[1]

Congress has power to issue money etc/ article 8 pp/5[2]

NO department of govt. has the right to hand over its functions to any other. You are merely illegal if you hand over right to issue money to, let us say, the Chief J Justice.[3]

 Frankie NEVER legally had these powers. Why go on compounding
    a felony or whatever.

    There was also some unadulterated CRAP about his wanting these
extra powers to balance exchanges etc/
            NUTTZ, nuts.
same section and pp/ "and to determine the value of foreign COIN."[4]
Congress has the power to FIX the exchange rate with foreign countries/
            JUST as has so successfully been done HERE/
you dont have to ask permission of Baruch and Rothschild or

go up to Sing Sing to tell Whitney.[5]

If congress SAYS the price of sterling is 4.70, it is illegal to buy above that.

    I wish you wd/ impeach the blighter/ but I suppose that is asking too much. Rosenfeld *** is *** a ***
                    [No closing]

1. Tinkham had been on the Committee on Election of President, Vice President, and Representatives since 14 January 1937, and would be reappointed 23 January 1939 (*Cong. Rec.* 14 Jan. 1937: 226; 23 Jan. 1939: 640).

2. Pound's reference to "article 8" of the Constitution is incorrect. The passage he has in mind is from Section 8 of Article I and reads as follows: "The Congress shall have power...To coin money, regulate the value thereof, and of foreign coin, and fix the Standard of Weights and Measures" (quoted in Kelly and Harbison 845).

3. The Chief Justice of the U. S. Supreme Court in 1939 was Charles Evans Hughes.

4. See n2, above.

5. Richard W. Whitney, a New York banker and stockbroker and ex-president of the New York Stock Exchange, had been convicted of embezzlement and sentenced to 5-10 years at Sing-Sing ("Whitney Receives 5 to 10").

69. Pound to Tinkham

[February 1939]

Am pintin out the coincidence of Presidential beardlessness
with DAMN'D ROT in the White House.

                    Dunno that they'll print it.

What we need is a national movement GROUNDED on John
ADAMS.

That cd/ start in Braintree.[1] I hope to visit that village.

                  ever

           hush, this not a signature
        for public use ["signature" missing]

1. Braintree (now Quincy), Massachusetts, was John Adams' birthplace. It was therefore an appropriate place to initiate a movement "grounded" on Adams.

70. Tinkham to Pound

February 23, 1939

Personal

My dear Ezra:
            Enclosed is a clipping from THE BOSTON
HERALD
of February 7 which I think you will be interested to see.
It certainly was most complimentary and kind of you to pro-
mote such publicity in Boston.[1]
            At the moment I am under a great deal of pres-
sure, which explains why I am not writing you more at length
at this time.
            I trust all goes well with you. Believe me,
with cordial personal regards,
                            Sincerely yours,
                    [signed] GEORGE HOLDEN TINKHAM
Mr. Ezra Pound
Via Marsala 12-5
Rapallo, Italy

encl.

1. In the newspaper item Pound suggests Tinkham for the Presidency ("Tinkham
Suggested for President").

71. Tinkham to Pound

May 15, 1939

My dear Mr. Pound
        I appreciate your kind proffer of
assistance.[1] Everything in Boston seems to be
moving satisfactorily at the moment and I
think Mr. Tinkham is making some progress in
adjusting his personal affairs there.
                With every good wish, I am
                        Sincerely yours,
        [signed] Grace C. Hamelin
                        Secretary to Mr. Tinkham
Mr. Ezra Pound
c/o Mr. F. S. Bacon[2]
80 Maiden Lane
New York, New York

1. Although it is not clear what kind of assistance Pound had "proffered," nor when he did so, he was to make what was probably a similar overture in November 1939. See Letter 81 (2 November 1939), where he offers to help in Tinkham's Boston office.
2. Francis S. Bacon was an American businessman and entrepreneur whom Pound admired. Having known him since 1910, Pound apparently stayed with Bacon during his 1939 visit (Stock, *Life* 90; Nicholls 30).

72. Tinkham to Pound

May 15, 1939

My dear Ezra:
        Sincere thanks for your several notes.
        Enclosed are letters of introduction
to several persons in Boston whom you might find
it interesting to see and to talk with.[1]
        I shall try to arrange a definite
appointment for you with Senator Borah.[2]
        With cordial good wishes, I remain
Sincerely yours,
[signed] GEORGE HOLDEN TINKHAM
Mr. Ezra Pound
c/o F. S. Bacon[3]
80 Maiden Lane
New York, New York

[encl.]

1. Tinkham wrote letters of introduction for Pound to Christian Herter, Massachusetts state representative; Leverett Saltonstall, governor of Massachusetts; Lincoln O'Brien, editor of the *Boston Evening Transcript*; and Frank W. Buxton, editor of the *Boston Herald*. He introduced Pound as "the distinguished poet and economist." In his letters to *both* of the influential newspaper editors, O'Brien and Buxton, Tinkham included the following sentence: "He [Pound] wished a letter of introduction to the most intelligent man in Boston; hence, this letter to you." Clearly, the congressman knew wherefrom his bread was buttered.
2. For note on Borah see Letter 10, n1.
3. For note on Bacon see Letter 71, n2.

73. Pound to Tinkham

[Handwritten note to Tinkham, late May or early June, 1939]

3301 P. St.

Waaal I give yr. salutations
to Borah this a.m.[1]
also seeing other lights,
& am dated up to see more,
& so forth.
    Washington very
    pleasant village or
    town. In fact only
habitable paart of the U.S.
known to me.
           yrz

1. It was probably during this interview with Borah that the senator placed his hand on Pound's shoulder and uttered the words that Pound records in Canto 84: "am sure I don't know what a man/like you would find to *do* here" ("On Resuming" 25).

74. Tinkham to Pound

June 5, 1939

Dear Ezra:

I am returning herewith the letter written by
Mr. James C. Grey of THE SUN[1] enclosed with your letter
of May 30.

I regret that my letters of introduction did
not reach you in time. In your note of May 13 you indicated that you wished your letters to be addressed to
you in care of Mr. F. S. Bacon, 80 Maiden Lane, New York,
and any telegrams sent to you in care of Mr. Theodore
Spencer, Eliot House, Cambridge, Massachusetts.[2]

I was much interested in your comments concerning your interview with Mr. Herter.[3]

I have delayed my acknowledgement of the receipt
of your letter of May 30 as I was expecting to see you
back in Washington this week.[4]

With cordial regards, I remain

Sincerely yours,

[signed] GEORGE HOLDEN TINKHAM

Ezra Pound, Esquire
c/o F. S. Bacon
80 Maiden Lane
New York, New York

[encl.]

1. Grey was literary editor of the *New York Sun* ("James C. Grey").
2. For note on Bacon see Letter 71, n2. Theodore Spencer was a Harvard
assistant professor of English, later to become Boylston Professor of Rhetoric
and Oratory ("Dr. T. Spencer").
3. Christian Herter was a Massachusetts state representative at the time.
4. The forwarding address on the accompanying envelope in the Beinecke file
shows that this letter eventually reached Pound c/o Professor A. P. Saunders at
Pound's *alma mater*, Hamilton College, Clinton, New York.

75. Tinkham to Pound

August 24, 1939

My dear Mr. Pound:

Your letter of August 14 was received today and is being forwarded at once to Mr. Tinkham, who is now in Boston.

With all good wishes, I am

Sincerely yours,

[signed] G.C. Hamelin

Secretary to Mr. Tinkham

Ezra Pound, Esquire
Via Marsala 12-5
Rapallo, Italy

76. Tinkham to Pound

At
Boston, Massachusetts
August 28, 1939

Ezra Pound, Esquire
Via Marsala 12-5
Rapallo, Italy

My dear Ezra:
Your communication of August 14 has been forwarded
to me here at Boston. I was much pleased to hear
from you.

I had heard some publication in an English paper
unidentified, of my resolutions for neutrality
which was filed in Congress some time ago.[1]
That is the only information of any publication
I have heard of. Of course, I have not seen a
copy.

Representative Martin, of course, will be Speaker
of the House if the Republicans have majority.[2]

It is very uncertain whether I go to Europe this
summer. I have so much disruption in my office here
in Boston, as I explained to you, I think.

My number one private secretary who was with me thirty
two years collapsed last November and it has put
a great deal of detail in front of me to be attended
to with some thorny questions.

I made reservation for the "Yankee Clipper" for
September 6, then postponed it until September 16.
I now am going to postpone it until the 15 or
20th of October. Whether I can go then is uncertain.

If there is war, as it is the only political "out"
for Roosevelt, he will do everything to get us in.
I predicted a course of events with that ending
to our Chief of Staff in April or May 1936.

When you receive this letter we shall know whether
there is to be war or peace. I have felt there

was to be no war but from our newspapers down to the last publication, I see about fifty-one percent chances for peace and forty-nine percent chances for war. The war, of course, will change the face of political things here very much.

Already the English propaganda is thundering.

With kindest personal regards, I remain
Sincerely yours,
[signed] GEORGE HOLDEN TINKHAM

1. Tinkham had offered two joint resolutions on neutrality: one "providing for the reassertion of a foreign policy of genuine neutrality for the United States" (*Cong. Rec.* 15 May 1939: 5561), and another "providing that the United States should maintain a policy of strict neutrality in Asia" (*Cong. Rec.* 4 Aug. 1939: 11117).
2. For note on Martin see Letter 38, n3.

77. Pound to Tinkham

2 Sept [1939]

Dear Uncle George
        There might be some utility in the
view that UNTIL the present kike government of England
is damn well licked the aryan population/especially
rural population of Eng/ will never get a square deal.

England where Habsburg Austria and Czarist Russia were in
I914
I mean in comparison with INTERNAL government of other
countries
      (except france).

The commutation of tithes in {HHH} England, i;e; what the
pore
bloody farmers had and could pay, into a money tax is
one of the dirtiest deals since the shitten Brits. cut off
the colonial paper money in I750 whatever. and thereby
drove the colonies to revolt.
        Some nice data re/ English relations to colonies
AND the Rothschild agents Ikleheimer, Morton and
Vandergould/
in W. Overholser's "History of Money in the U.S."
60 pages, 25 cents/ Progress Publishing Concern, Libertyville
Illinois. Best thing I have read or reread in a long time.
though Rota's Storia delle banche has some good hits.[1]

            ever yours

  [Bli]thering idiocy of England's fake position is that if
  [Rus]sian regiments went in to Poland, Eng wd/ be in
  *** bought to take on the Rhoobloodyushuns.[2]

---

1. Ikleheimer, Morton and Van der Gould was a New York bank (Pound, "Gold
and Work" 339). Ettore Rota (1883-1958) was an Italian historian and professor
of medieval and modern history at the University of Pavia. He co-edited *Nuovo
Rivista Storia* and wrote *Le Origini del Risorgimento* ("Rota").
2. England had just signed a treaty with Poland, on August 25, whereby she
would come to Poland's defense in the event of an attack by Germany. The
treaty did not require that England defend Poland against any other aggressor,
including Russia ("'British Treaty with Poland").

78.   Pound to Tinkham

I2 Sept [1939]

Yaaaas, damnBit, My dear Uncle George
        I know Martin will be speaker IF etc.
What I want to know is: Are the republicans putting up a
candidate with some horse sense, OR "a stuffed shirt"
as Senator W. said they wd/do "and git licked"??[1]

I cd. find it in my heart to wish the demmys wd/nominate
SENATOR Bankhead (not the other one) I dont believe he
likes the Roosenstein = Cohen combination much better than we
do.[2]

Wyndham Lewis has got to Canada.[3] I have told him to paint
your portrait (by force if necessary). The job ought to be
done. You dont want a chromo lithograph.

As fer Martin, wot I want (indiscretely) to know IS
what the hell is he up to INSIDE Massachusetts. if anything.
These are the details. etc//

I forget whether I told you of my lunch at the Polish
Embassy last May. Potocki said they wd/fight with or
WITHOUT
England's help.[4] I naturally was telling him England's help
was no bloody use. I spose he may see that by NOW.

Whether the damn brits/YET see the need of putting
some of their farm land back into cultivation, gorr noze.

One farmer being worth at least 40 usurers to a blockaded
country
and no war yet ever won by taxes.

I believe the Vivaldi week is being held in Siena, at least
no news yet of its being called off.[5]
I shall then go to Venice (3I0 San Gregorio), till the
Middle of Oct. and then return here; unless something
unforeseen
happens.

Not one word of sense in Brit. and French papers/ or rather
    yes, a few. and no news of what people outside newswyper

control are doing or thinking in either country.

I keep on recommending Overholser's sixty pages on History of Money in U.S.

very clear on British prohibition of money to colonies in I750 that counting for much more than stamp tax etc.
and much more interesting in relation to history of past 5 years same old goddam wheeze.

                              yours ever

Proofs of my resume of Chinese history (economic) and J. Adams are coming thru from London. I dont know whether my
corrected galleys are getting back to Faber (pubrs)?[6]

1. For note on Martin see Letter 38, n3. For note on "Senator W." (Wheeler), see Letter 38, n4.
2. For note on Senator Bankhead, see Letter 15, n9. The "other one" was William Brockman Bankhead, the U. S. Representative from Alabama who was then Speaker of the House of Representatives (1936-40). ("Bankhead, William Brockman"). Benjamin V. Cohen (1894-1983) was a lawyer and advisor to President Roosevelt on New Deal legislation. He had been counsel to the American zionists at the London and Paris peace conferences after World War I ("Cohen").
3. Percy Wyndham Lewis (1884-1957) was the British writer and painter and friend of Pound ("Lewis, Percy Wyndham").
4. Count Jerzy Potocki (1889-1961) was the Polish ambassador to the United States (1936-40). Previously, he had been ambassador to Rome (1933) ("Jerzy Potocki, 72, is Dead").
5. Since 1936 Pound had been organizing a series of Vivaldi concerts and lectures in an effort to revive interest in the Italian composer (Stock, *Life* 337-38).
6. Noel Stock reports that the proofs of Pound's Chinese cantos were ready "by November" (Stock, *Life* 369). According to Pound's account in this letter to Tinkham, he had already been correcting them as early as September.

79. Tinkham to Pound

September 30, 1939

My dear Ezra:
         I hope you will excuse my not writing to you sooner in reply to your several communications. I have had considerable difficulty in my Boston office and have been obliged to spend a good deal of time there with an office organization not so good as formerly. Here in Washington, since September 1, I have been receiving more than five hundred letters a day bearing upon the so-called neutrality proposal.[1] Only one and one-half per cent of these letters are in favor of the proposed repeal of the arms embargo provision. Many other members of Congress are receiving the same character of mail; however, for some unknown reason, the Administration seems to have control of the Senate and I am afraid that may mean control of the House, in the final analysis, for repeal. Nothing, however, is really certain. In my opinion, the repeal of the arms embargo provision would be a long step on the road to war. There is a powerful feeling among the members of both the House and Senate that the American people generally are opposed to United States entry into war, just as they were in 1914. In my opinion, the President will stop at nothing finally to involve us.
         Enclosed is a letter which I am sending to residents of my district who are writing me on this subject.
         So far as the 1940 presidential situation is concerned, everything is inchoate. Vandenberg has taken a strong position against the repeal of the embargo and Taft has taken a strong position the other way.[2]
         So far as Martin is concerned, his hands are full with the legislative situation here. I do not think he is doing anything in Massachusetts for the time being.[3]
         The English and French military situation, with the communique out of Berlin September 29 giving details of the new

Soviet Russia-Germany accord concluded at Moscow, is certainly
historic and very portentous for Europe, if not for the world.[4]
English realists must be profoundly pessimistic.

With kindest personal regards, I remain

Sincerely yours,

[signed] GEORGE HOLDEN TINKHAM

Ezra Pound, Esquire
Via Marsala 12-5
Rapallo, Italy

[encl.]

[Following is a copy of the letter Congressman Tinkham sent to his constituents who had written him about the neutrality proposal.]

Sincere thanks for your communication of recent date. I was very pleased to hear from you.

For years I have opposed any political commitments by the United States in Europe or in any other continent, and I had much to do with drawing the present neutrality act. I am wholly opposed to the United States entering the European war and am wholly opposed to any step in that direction. I certainly believe that the repeal of the arms embargo would be in that direction and would mean war for the United States in the end. Although the President talks peace, in my opinion, his purpose is war.

With all good wishes, I remain

Sincerely yours,

[signed] GEORGE HOLDEN TINKHAM

1. In his desire to aid Britain and France after they had been drawn into the war with Germany's invasion of Poland, Roosevelt had proposed that the arms embargo provisions of the Neutrality Act of 1935 be repealed. The embargo was in fact repealed by November 1939 (Burns 394-97), much to the dismay of isolationists like Tinkham.
2. For note on Vandenberg see Letter 15, n1. Robert Alphonso Taft (1889-1953), the son of President William Howard Taft, was U.S. Senator from Ohio (1939-53). He would seek the Presidency himself in four successive elections from 1940 ("Taft, Robert Alphonso").
3. For note on Martin see Letter 38, n3.
4. The initial Nazi-Soviet pact of 24 August 1939, which affirmed mutual neutrality and nonaggression, had virtually guaranteed Hitler's invasion of Poland on September 1, which in turn provoked the Anglo-French declarations

of war on Germany. The pact also provided for separate German and Soviet partitioning of eastern Europe, which opened the door for Soviet as well as German aggression. The subsequent agreements to which Tinkham refers made the two powers, in effect, allies against Britain and France (Keleher 1433-36; Tolischus, "Germany Jubilant"). Tinkham's assessment of the "portentous" atmosphere was accurate.

80. Tinkham to Pound

October 19, 1939

My dear Mr. Pound:

I regret there has been so long a delay in sending you the enclosed letter which Mr. Tinkham dictated on September 30. The work of the office has been considerably retarded by my enforced absence because of the critical illness of my father, who the doctors seemed to believe could not recover. However, I am glad to say that he has rallied and that his condition at present is considerably better.

With all good wishes, I am

Sincerely yours,

[signed] G. C. Hamelin

Secretary to Mr. Tinkham

Ezra Pound
Via Marsala 12-5
Rapallo, Italy

[encl.][1]

1. Ms. Hamelin's letter was a cover letter for Tinkham's of 30 September 1939 (see Letter 79).

81. Pound to Tinkham

2 Nov. [1939]

Dear Uncle George

        I am not interested in what Frankie WANTS
but in what one can STOP him from getting.[1]
If yr/ Boston office is being a nuissance why not put ME
into it. I know you picture me floatin' round in a gondola
plucking water lilies ete/etc/
but my favorite theologian Scotus Erigina defined sin as; a
LAPSE from reality.[2]
        Mebbe a little political close up wd/ be
valuable experience for one still young but not exactly
in first blush of jejune innocence.
Young Jas[3] motored me along that river front; my life has not
been one long sunday in sunday school, though doubtless etc.
I am IG GURUNT and how of the sidelights of Bastun.
        I make this suggestion just to indicate that I can
at moments be a serious character.
        In the interim I wish you wd. converse with Sam
Pryor.[4] He struck me a bright lad. And if you and he and
    Hank Mencken[5] cd/ agree on ANYthing, I imagine I cd.
swallow it. I am convinced people stay too much INSIDE their
own little circles.
       You by now have got USED to seeing life from the
majority side/ fortune of the I0th district.
Pryor was aware that a MINORITY has to get votes FROM the
other side.

                               possible
       Parenthesis; my idea of my own utility
in the Boston office is that at present EVERYBODY in that
office and around it knows everything about everyone else.
I can conceive the USE of a nonconducting substance.

I am not so much interested in what Joe has omitted
because of business in the National Capital, as in what may have
happened in Mass. itself: while J.M. is otherwise occupied.[6]

Of course at this distance I live in blank ignorance of
local detail.

Vandenberg was YOUR pick. I can NOT see him as
INTERESTING

the kind of left wingers that I can contact.
I thought he had the edge on Bridges recently, apropos
Europe.
I think you thought me right about Taft, last April.
The other younger men I met in Washington were surprised at
my liking Taft at all.

I didn't get down to economics with Bridges.[7] I liked him
very much and he was O.K. on Europe. then.
                    //
Frankie's frontiers were then on the Rhine/Hitler smacked him.
No no muvver's boye must bbbbleeeed. Molitoff has just
kicked Mr Jewsfeldt in the breeches.[8]

Eden as I am suggesting have managed to win the war
        and co/
                            for Russia without winning it
                            for england.[9]

The american jews may find themselves without a landing place
on the West coast. of Europe.

There is a steady flow of quotation from Swedish and Dutch
    papers showing that Europe is gradually awakening to the
non European nature of yitts.

Of course fer me and Stoddard ANY suggestion that Chinamen
[don't?]
differ from Norwegians or Portageese will soon become
suspect.[10]
        I see me old acquaintance Gorham Munson is writing
against anti=semitism. Despite his admired Maj. Douglas being
a good healthy anti=yitt.[11]

The intelligentzia in Amurikaaa will shortly be discussing
RACE etc// and the difference in Chinese endocrine reactions
to Welsh hormone distillation etc.

If gawd loved England, they wd. send Neville[12] to an home fer
the senile and shoot the rest of the cabinet, but they
are as a race 90% docile and accustomed to being conquered
at intervals.

What the american GOOF thinks England is going to WIN [in]
this war, gorr alone knows.

And then the jews felt/ that they must leave Mr. Roosevelt.

God alone knows why the Baltimore Sun and N.Y. Sun are both pro Roosevelt. They OUGHT not to be.

Tremaine is another damn good man. Pryor OUGHT to be made to see that he has got to AUGMENT the republican and/or
anti Roosevelt forces.[13]

Must have SOME PRESS. must be some place to write IN/ some means of communicating with the public.

I keep hammering on PUT CONGRESS ON THE RADIO.

But if after flooding the Supreme court/ the discussion of Neutrality IN CONGRESS can be plugged by a hat trick... then damn it, even radio isn't ENOUGH. Party must have newspapers. Capitol Daily OUGHT NOT to have been allowed to stop.
         Greenwich Time?? what's it up to?
         that is at least local in strong republican town
could be built up as national organ IF IF IF etc.[14]
               and so forth.
               [No closing]

[The following note to Tinkham's secretary, G. C. Hamelin, accompanies this letter.]

Dear Miss Hamelin
         I am sorry your father has been so ill.
Glad to hear of his recovery.

You might let me know whether Overholser has sent in his little history of money.
If not do for god's sake order a copy. Trust me for the 25 cents it costs. I will repay.

History of Money in the U.S. / by Willis Overholser/
      Public Service Buildings, Libertyville, Illinois.
               you get it from Overholser himself.
and see that Mr Tinkham looks at pages 27/8 and 44/49.
say I said so, to both Mr O/ and Mr T/
               [No closing]

1. Pound is referring to Tinkham's claim, expressed in his letter of 30 September 1939 (see Letter 79), that Roosevelt wants the U. S. to enter the war.

2. Scotus Erigina (c.810-c.877) was a medieval philosopher and theologian ("Erigina").

3. "Young Jas" may refer to James Laughlin. Cf. Letter 27, including n3.

4. Samuel F. Pryor, Jr., had been Republican National Committee member from Connecticut in 1936 and would become vice chair for 1940 ("Republican Group").

5. Henry Lewis (H. L.) Mencken (1880-1956) was an American author, critic, and editor ("Mencken").

6. "Joe" and "J. M." refer to Representative Joseph Martin of Massachusetts. Cf. Letter 38, n3.

7. For note on Vandenberg see Letter 15, n1; for note on Taft see Letter 79, n2; and for note on Bridges see Letter 38, n1.

8. "Molitoff" is Vyacheslav Mikhailovitch Molotov (1890-1986), who was the Russian diplomat who negotiated the nonaggression treaty with Germany's Joachim von Ribbentrop ("Molotov"; and cf. Letter 79, n4). In his report on foreign affairs to the Supreme Soviet on 31 October, Molotov criticized Roosevelt for giving moral support to Finland, and for repealing the arms embargo. He claimed that U. S. policy would "not...weaken war and hasten its termination, but...intensify, aggravate and protract it" ("Points"). "Jewsfeldt" is one of Pound's many anti-semitic references to Roosevelt; by referring to Roosevelt in this manner, he meant to suggest the President's collusion with Jewish bankers and financiers as well as attribute to the President himself a Jewish ancestry.

9. For note on Eden see Letter 12, n2. Given the antisemitic context of Pound's accusation about Eden's winning the war for Russia rather than England, he may be thinking of what he perceived as Eden's Jewish/banking connections, but the implications are hardly clear.

10. Theodore Lathrop Stoddard (1883-1950) was an American writer on social, international, economic, and racial subjects ("Stoddard"). Given Pound's view on racial differences, the sentence would make more sense if it read "...Chinamen *don't* differ...." (my italics).

11. Gorham Bert Munson (1896-1969) was an American author and critic who edited *New Democracy* (1933-39) ("Munson"). Pound is probably referring to Munson's "Anti-Semitism: A Poverty Problem," published in *Christian Century*, 4 October 1939. For note on Douglas see Letter 8, n7.

12. For note on Neville Chamberlain, see Letter 65, n2.

13. "Tremaine" is probably Morris Sawyer Tremaine (1871-1941), the state comptroller of New York (1927-41) (Kimpel and Eaves 308).

14. The *Capitol Daily* had stopped publishing earlier in 1939. The issue for May 9 included an article by Pound, "Ezra Pound on Gold, War and National Money" (Gallup, C1509). Pound had published an article in *Greenwich Time*, on July 13, entitled "The Cabinet of a Dream, and Congress Should Go on the Air" (Gallup, C1512).

82. Pound to Tinkham

7 Nov. [1939]

Dear Uncle George
                              I asked you one very delicate question
last spring, and you answered "No; but they could be used."
Now living in awtistik an licherary etc/ milieu in Europe
I have not been much with American masons. But I shd/ say
the last thing any American mason wd/ think of, and
still more strongly the last thing he wd/ tolerate wd/ be
the idea of the U.S.A. taking orders from a gang of kikes
in Belgium or Paris. WHATEVER high falutin and easterin
top dressing they used.

An I leave it at that. In Venice you said "I'm goin' to
do a job on that feller."
                              //
Lincoln was shot. Huey Long was shot. I dont know
what is back of the last assault on Mosley.[1] Certainly not
british workers; in Glasgow they are demanding nationalization
of
mines, and pasting hakenkreuz on 4I shop windows/as the
brief paragraph says "the perbloody=lice suspect an
antiyitt association" I spose it was on jew shops.
                              I {get} see quotes from Scandinavian papers
etc. the idea of the jew hoping the european white man will
exterminate himself seems fairly well diffused.
                              Any idea as to Molitoff's ethnic background?[2]

The one bit of inside news that I trust, was that
antisemitism was coming up in Russia. peasants loathing
small officials, bureaucrats; all of which had got into
hands of jews.

Friends of Tremaine's whom I found onto a lot of stuff
(jawed with him on the boat coming back most days)
thought republicans cd. win on straight anti=semitic platform.
I was also assured by another chap, young but of
"large" family connections, that "Jack wd. throw 'em out"
(meaning Garner, who cert. is NOT a pick with reformers
like yr/ obt. nevvy Ez.P.)[3]

I dont think ANYone in Europe looks on the abrogation of
embargo

as motivated by anything save rank lust for profits, due
to bloodshed.

The english whom I know are of all sorts of opposed groups
but NONE of 'em believes in this war. Mosley has been
absolutely consistent. Friendship with Germany and fight
like hell if they attack the Brit. Empire.
                    (which dont include embezzling
the mandates from the archi=rotten and utterly stunk League
of Nations.)

The fools and naive criminals have fairly exposed themselves
in a book by Clarence Streit (not Straight) Union Now
pubd. last march.

All the punks on that bill. Steed, Nic But. Nor Angell, Ed Grigg
etCETERA[4]

                    yrs.

1. Sir Oswald Mosley (1896-1980) was the leader of the British Union of Fascists,
organized in 1932; his open support of Nazism and Fascism led to his
imprisonment in England during the war (1940-43) ("Mosley"). While Mosley
had been hit by a thrown stick at a demonstration in Wilmslow, near
Manchester, on 5 November 1939 ("Attacks on Sir O. Mosley"), he had been
assaulted on prior occasions as well. His head had been "gashed open by a brick"
at a political meeting in early November, 1937, and on 12 July 1936 a bullet
penetrated the window of his car – the only "genuine attempt" on his life
(Skidelsky 415,417n).
2. If Pound suspected that Molotov was Jewish, he was wrong. Molotov had
recently become commissar for foreign affairs, replacing Maxim Litvinov, who, as
a Jew, would not be an effective negotiator with the Nazis during the
nonaggression talks ("Molotov").
3. For note on Tremaine see Letter 81, n13. John Nance ("Jack") Garner (1868-
1967) was Vice President of the United States (1933-41) ("Garner").
4. Clarence Kirshman Streit (1896-1986) was an American journalist whose book,
Union Now (1939), advocated a federal union of North Atlantic democracies
("Streit"). Henry Wickham Steed (1871-1956), a British historian and journalist,
was foreign editor of *The Times* and had directed Allied propaganda during
World War I ("Steed"). Edward Grigg (1879-1955) was a British journalist and
politician who had once edited *The Times* and *The Outlook* ("Altrincham Dies").
For note on Angell see Letter 8, n9. The opinions of these men were expressed
in Streit's book.

83. Tinkham to Pound

November 27, 1939

Dear Mr. Pound:
        Your letter of November 7 to Congressman Tinkham
has just been received. Mr. Tinkham has gone South for
a month's vacation and I am under instructions to forward
no mail to him. I am therefore holding your letter here
for his attention when he returns.
                        Sincerely yours,
                [signed] G. C. Hamelin
                        Secretary to Mr. Tinkham

Ezra Pound
Via Marsala 12-5
Rapallo, Italy

84. Pound to Tinkham

II Jan [1940]

Dear Uncle George
I enclose a copy of a petition to the
Supreme Court which concerns a young friend of yours.

I believe the procedure correct in cases where the Constitution
is involved. In any case it is the second time in ten years
that attention (my attention) has been drawn to state dept.
rulings which violate that particular clause of the constitution.
In this case the consulate tells me that the State Dept
was against the ruling and the Dept. of Labour insisted and
went to the Attorney General
who OUGHT to know the
constitution, but considering the present tendency to violate
it in all depts. and cases of course he may not. In which
case he ought to be TOLD.

I dont imagine Sis Perkins is in a jew plot to make my
life miserable, but we cd. do with a few I00% aryan citizens
just to maintain at least a minority.[1]
2.
I wish you wd. converse with Sam Pryor[2] for about I5 minutes.
3.
I wish, procedure permitting that you wd. shortly rise in the
House and offer the following few and I believe chosen words.

BE IT MOVED THAT the debates in this House and those
henceforth
in the Senate be immediately transmitted by radio so that
any citizen wishing to know what his representatives are
doing will have opportunity to same while they are doing it.[3]

I have private advice from Connecticut that there has
been quite a bit of favourable talk re/ this suggestion.

Anyhow it wd. remind the denizens of yr/
presence.
4.
Goddamit, whether you mean to oblige or not, I believe the
Party ought to think out or have thunk out FOR THEM
some sort of 20 year policy that they cd. at
least appear to believe in or agree on.

I believe the American system of govt. is worth restoring.

Yrs devotedly

By the way the consul was deeply grateful for another little bright deed of YOURS, that of trying to get veterans' wives decently treated after the last war.

Hang it all if you will CONCEAL all yr/ assets in the Congressional Record, what the hell is one to do.

Europe is very interesting at the moment.

1. Frances Perkins was Secretary of Labor; the Attorney General was Frank Murphy.
2. For note on Pryor see Letter 81, n4.
3. Tinkham did not raise this issue in Congress.

85. Tinkham to Pound

February 14, 1940

<u>Personal</u>

My dear Ezra:
      I thought you would be interested in the enclosed
page from the February 13 issue of THE WASHINGTON
POST with
the three articles, "Unhappy Chameleon" by Mark Sullivan,[1]
"The
Republican Nomination For President" and one in rel-
tion to Mexico.
      There is plenty to hear, and a great deal of
froth and foolishness, framed in by the greatest uncertainty
in every direction with a psychopathic hysteric presiding
over all.
      With cordial good wishes, I remain
Sincerely yours,
[signed] GEORGE HOLDEN TINKHAM

Mr. Ezra Pound
Via Marsala 12-5
Rapallo, Italy

encl.

1. Mark Sullivan, an American journalist with isolationist views, was a frequent
critic of the Roosevelt Administration ("Mark Sullivan").

86. Tinkham to Pound

February 29, 1940

My dear Ezra:

Last Sunday I read the enclosed article in the New York Times Book Review in which you will note your name appears. I thought it would interest you.[1]

With cordial good wishes, I remain

Sincerely yours,

[signed] GEORGE HOLDEN TINKHAM

Ezra Pound, Esquire
Via Marsala 12-5
Rapallo, Italy

Encl.

1. The article must have been from a different issue of the *New York Times Book Review* or from a different newspaper of the same date. I find no reference to Pound in the *Book Review* Tinkham refers to.

87. Pound to Tinkham

Via Marsala I2-5 Rapallo 22 March I940

Dear Uncle George
          It seems that Rothschild in time of Napoleon ran
the Austrian mailservice and opened letters to get financial etc/
information. If you are lookin' fer readin' matter try McNair
Wilson's "Mind of Napoleon" (omitting his religious kinks the
story is good).[1] Giornale di Genova this a/m mentions yr
remarks.
I dont know whether I have any news that you haven't seen.
Finland
equals anglo/canad/ nickel. Mond (dirty Frankfort yitt family
alias Lord Melchett, Imperial Chemicals, Manchester Guardian.
Believe the nickel co/ banks with Hambros, whereof is Astor a
director, and unless something has shifted Astor equals the
London
"Times".[2]

French papers in state of diliquescence? Dear friend who has
been
thinking me crazy for I5 years because I insisted france was on
the
down, finally convinced yesterday by being shown copy of Le
Journal
(back page of six page paper) full of weak jokes, colour pictures
french and english about "tommis". but WEAK, compare it with
Le
Rire of 30 years go. HELL.// I think I said last spring that the
internal french show looked to me like a shindy between the
yidd
(late en[t]rants) and the old original gang of Necker's swine in
the Banque. Very clear article few days ago said the sham
reform
under Blum was only the finance gang ousting the armaments
gang.
Renaud, I think, mere pimp for London. Both countries
governed by
national enemies aim to crush all the decent life of gentry, or
anyone with income from 400 to 2000 sterling/ and leave whole
thing
in jew hands[3]...continental press, outside france, more and more
open in publication views coinciding with what mine have been.
By

the way, have you seen the nice preamble to young Voorhis H. R. 8080.[4] Could anybody hook it OUT of committee with a boat hook?

yrz

emendment ought to remove the words which follow "immediately" on
p. 5. 9 to 12 million unemployed ought to be enough emergency without waiting for external complications.

1. For note on McNair Wilson see Letter 12, n7.
2. For note on Mond see Letter 41, n8. Waldorf Astor, second Viscount Astor (1879-1952), was proprietor of *The Observer* but not of *The Times*. He was, however, a close friend of the editor of *The Times*, Geoffrey Dawson ("Astor"). Apart from his newspaper and financial interests, Astor would have incurred Pound's contempt for being a strong supporter of the League of Nations.
3. Jacques Necker (1732-1804) was a French statesman and international financier who was director general of finances in pre-revolutionary France ("Necker"). For note on Blum see Letter 8, n5. Jean Renaud was a French communist party deputy ("Beat French Red Deputy" 4).
4. Congressman Voorhis' H.R. 8080, the National Credit for Defense Act, was intended to create credit "in a non-interest-bearing debt-free form" so that war could be financed without incurring a huge debt. In his "preamble" to the bill he said that wars are traditionally financed through loans from the private banking system – a claim that was one of Pound's favorite themes (*Cong. Rec.* 22 Jan. 1940, App.: 292)

88. Pound to Tinkham

23 March [1940]

Dear Unkle George
        Here is the clipping. I hope you get it.
Letter takes 3 weeks from the U.S. and apparently 2 to get there.
I spose they lie round on the decks at Gibralter
proclaimin the freedom of the seas and the power of the American
navy. And nobody but us old enough to remember Decatur etc.[1]
I enc/ also General Grant's picture as he mightn't have expected
to find it. Miss H.[2] might let me know if it reaches you.

I dunno if it is LEGAL for congressmen to read poetry
(I know they get funny stuff printed in the "leave to print"
parts of the record, on the occasions of monuments to
confederate veterans etc.) and I dont in the least care whether
you consider it as poetry or as telegraphic notes, but
I am sending you Cantos 52/7I

A little tenderness shown on P/II/I2 where I had alluded to
ye olde bankinge firme may catch yr/ eye. Well Faber
is a game sport to have published it, anyhow.[3]

Members used to quote LATIN authors, I spose because there was
something IN THEM, apart from birds and flowyers.
And I have been quoted in the Belgian chamber, but that
wasn't my poetry, only an essay on Les Wallonais.

If you can stand the choppy delivery (and damn it IF one is
gettin the gist of I2 folios onto I00 pages, one has to cut
something) I am free to doubt if there is a quicker way of
Meetin Mr J. Adams. 62/7I The Chinese Cantos 52/6I
at least show it didn't all start last tuesday morning. Banzai
Ouan Soui, may you live for ten thousand years.
                [No closing]

1. Stephen Decatur (1779-1820) was an American naval officer who, in 1815, exacted agreements with Algiers and other Barbary states to protect American commercial shipping from harrassment and tribute ("Decatur").
2. Grace C. Hamelin, Congressman Tinkham's Washington secretary.

3. Cantos 52-71 were published by Faber on 28 January 1940 (Stock, *Life* 375)
The "tenderness" to which Pound refers is five lines in Canto 52 that Faber had
edited out, replacing them with black bars (*Cantos LII-LXXI* 12-13).

89. Pound to Tinkham

23 Marzo [1940]

Damn it all,
I have just wasted 40 cents on an overweight air mail
and I keep on thinkin'.
I think you ought to RUN. I don't believe it wd. kill
you. You'd spend less wrath matter and nervous energy making
a sane decision now and again, than in losin yr/ temper
over the idiotic decisions (or indecisions) of others.

All right, Vandendewey and all the rest of 'em. Frankie will
roll 'em up like he roll up ole "frozen Jack" Garner.[1]
They "aint GOT IT."
yrz

1. The composite referenee, "Vandendewey," refers to Michigan Senator Arthur
Hendrick Vandenberg and New York politician Thomas Edmund Dewey, both
potential Republican candidates for the Presidency in 1940. Cf. Letter 15, n1,
and Letter 38, n2. For note on Garner see Letter 82, n3.

90. Pound to Tinkham

5 April [1940]

Dear Uncle George
            I have at last got round to readin' an
ORTHODOX eee or eel=conomist (D.R. Dewey Financial
History of
the U.S.¹) and as a study of the unconscious he sure is a
corker. Standard text book since 1903/ 12th edtn. 1939

And wot he LEAVES OUT is a marvel.

However on p/ 377 he sez; legal tender circulation (of
greenbacks) is STILL only 346,681,000 as WUZ in {1875}.
                                                    1878
Is this possible, or does it merely mean that he hasn't
revised that page since the edtn. of 1903.

"volume of legal=tender circulation is still current"

Wot is yr/ CANDID opinion of John Sherman of Ohio?
M/C. from 1855/ senator and Sec/ of Treasury under Hayes.
and so far as Dewey records never jailed.

            cordially yrs

Thanks for clipping/ az matr/ of fact. It was not me, but
Joyce's megalomania forbids him admit that a mere hebe doctor
from N.Y. led him to the dental chair.²

1. Davis Rich Dewey (1858-1942), the brother of John Dewey, was an economist
("Dewey, Davis Rich").
2. Cf. Letter 86, n1.

91. Pound to Tinkham

7 April [1940]

G.H. Tinkham M.C.

Dear Uncle George
          EF the guvvyment dont know wot to do with its
money, I suggest the appropriation of a million to erect a
column of INFAMY to John Sherman
                    I note his actions from 1863/
as they say here "poco chiro", a bit shadowy.
The timing of some of the silver activities very queer.

Of course silver just another damn special commodity, a special
interest inserted for end of a group, and obfuscating all
thought about honest money for at least 20 years/

Do you know any published work giving the dirt on Sherman,
or any way of getting the profs/ and stewd/dents to investigatin
it. Did I say I had jined the Acad/ of Political or Polecatical
and Social Science/ dunno if there is any human material
there. Old Sine Butler is fallin foul of Damrosch inside
the supposedly intellectual tea = pots of the "Ac(bloody and
godsave)
CAD(you bet)amy and the Insteroot.[1] (Which latter if not
propter at least post my incivilities has at last pubd/ a
statement of its resources. Butler being illegal, I gather.
Waaal that all vurry small peas.

                    devvotedly yrs

INsufficient use being made, for campaign purposes, of the
TRADITION of the Republican party as friend of working man
and defence of purchasing power of his wage.

ANY party that goes fer to create or enlarge debt, is a
Usurers' party. and HOW.

1. Walter Johannes Damrosch (1862-1950) was an American composer and
conductor, and was president of the National Institute of Arts and Letters
("Damrosch"). For note on Butler see Letter 1, n2.

92. Pound to Tinkham

18 April [1940]

Dear Uncle George
                Is there any printed, or unprinted or
whatsoever or wheretofore available or unavailable LIST of
the people from whom "the administration" has BOUGHT its
goddam gold at fancy prices?

As fer your doing that job you promised.[1] If you don't
start soon it will be tardy. But in any case send me whatever
available
tables tablets or jibblets exist. FROM WHOM wuz the damn
stuff purr/chased? Over the peeriod from 1933 or 34 till the
NOW.
                [No closing]

---

1. The "job" Tinkham had "promised" may be the same one Pound mentions obscurely in Letter 82 ("In Venice you said 'I'm goin' to do a job on that feller.' ").

93.   Tinkham to Pound

May 16, 1940

My dear Mr. Pound:
    With reference to your letter of April 20, I
take pleasure in enclosing a self-explanatory communication
which has just been received from the Treasury Department.
The publications mentioned therein are being mailed to
you today under separate cover.[1]
    With all good wishes, I remain
                            Sincerely yours,
                    [signed] G. C. Hamelin
                        Secretary to Mr. Tinkham
Ezra Pound, Esquire
Via Marsala 12-5
Rapallo, Italy

1. If the "April 20" reference is accurate, the letter itself has been lost. However, it must have contained a request similar to that of 18 April 1940 (see Letter 92). The "self-explanatory communication" Ms. Hamelin refers to is a letter to Mr. Tinkham from the Director of the Mint. The "publications mentioned therein" are reports of the Secretary of the Treasury for fiscal years 1932-39, and annual reports of the Director of the Mint for corresponding years.

94. Pound to Tinkham

2I May [1940]

Dear Uncle George
        I suppose France and England may wake up
some day to the nature of back=seat driving from the U.S.

In the mean time IS the Rep/ party gaga? or is it only
foreign press reports. Frankie's LAST cinema act, the
"coalition party or cabinet!!!!!

Certain subsequent to my suggestion for a republican campaign
the possibly megalomania on my part to suppose he has heard
either of me or my suggestion.

ANYhow if the republicans are bought off by the inclusion [of]
two of the worst idiots that ever got into the republican
party, it is or OUGHT (of a right etc.)to be the END of
pea time.[1]

I see also that Mr. Lindbergh etc///[2]

Thank God there are still five months before the peepul go
to the poles. lets hope it wont be with a capital P.

        yrz

1. In the interest of national defense and to ensure a smooth transition between administrations, should the Republicans win in November, Roosevelt had decided to create a "coalition" or bipartisan cabinet, including Republican Secretaries of the Navy and War. Such a cabinet, according to Arthur Krock, writing in the *New York Times* on May 21, would "isolate national defense measures from politics and...coordinate procurement and production in a wholly nonpartisan way." The two "worst idiots that ever got into the republican party" were Alfred Landon (War) and Frank Knox (Navy), the 1936 Republican running-mates. Landon, however, would not consider the post unless Roosevelt publicly renounced a third term. The President, unwilling to make the disclaimer, named Henry L. Stimson instead (Burns 424). As a former member of the Taft and Hoover cabinets, and as a staunch internationalist, Stimson was probably no more acceptable to Pound than Landon was.
2. In his reference to Charles A. Lindbergh (1902-1974), the world famous aviator, Pound is probably alluding to current speculations about his running for vice-president on the Republican ticket, along with Wendell Willkie. Father Coughlin's *Social Justice* had done him "the unsolicited honor" of backing him for the office ("Lindbergh").

95. Pound to Tinkham

Rapallo, via Marsala I2-5 24 July I940

(penult)

Dear Uncle George: Thanks for yrs/ of 24th May. arrived
I know not via Portugal or Japan, but NO thanks to Hull's
diplomacy, which has, I take it reached a new low without even
a Paraguay, Uruguay or Bolivia to provide him a Benes or
Tafari.[1]

Re/ the sheeny, his reeport is what I had assumed.[2] The public
curiosity is not invited, and IF any information were available it
wd/ be unrevealing. a start for investigation, not a statement of
pregnant fact.

The NEXT step to see whether "if not available FOR
DISTRIBUTION"
the record is there at all. Payne or one of Stoddard's friends
ought to go down to the treasury, with introd from you or some
authority and ask to see the books. In the mean time, as Miss
Hamelin has a sense of humour I suggest you send her over
there,
she shd/ enter AS IF prepared for steady research, and ask to
see
the record. Not for what shd/ cd/ get from the ledgers in half an
hour, but for her perception of facial expression of those asked
for the facts.[3]

Have had good letter from D.R. Dewey (not master Tommy)
but Americ.
Econ. Review (Financial History of U. S.)[4] also confirming my
suppositions re/ lacunae or rather lack of ANY serious history
of
the U.S. financial and econ. affairs.
/// as to Willkie, subject to yr/ correction, he is (?) the man
who
slept for 20 years/ I shd/ not welcome the Atlantic Monthly in
the
White House, and as it has run "crap for the utilities" I dont
suppose Rip van Wendle's articles were tempered to please that
dirty piece of work Sedgwick, but rather that Willkie is the papa
of my NON=cousin Arthur p. etc. in short the fount of blah.[5]

I shd/ favour the dems/ on hope that the good gawd wd/ take

Franklin to that fitting receptacle, Abraham's bosom SOON, where F.
wd. be racially at home, with his old cronies and their 24 elders, and the cow that laid the golden calf...that wd. leave Wallace[6]
...wonder wd/ he have the guts to sack Morgenthaustein?? I wonder
in fact what Wheeler's monetary views are.[7] Did you get my article
on the gold purchases?[8] and did you show it to Wheeler?

Sounds as if the worst dems/ had been deloused. However, I shall
hold off till I get more news/ Attack on the four billion boodle shd/ be intensified/ in ANY case/ whichever way the mule jumps. If
Willkie WONT use the facts of my article, damn him. If Wallace can't??? in any case lets hope there may be a very small majority for either undesirable candidate. Frankie dont look like a FOURTH
term. Willkie's chance only on people voting against not FOR anything. (or do I err?)

I am not set in my mind, as haven't had enough data. But the gold
wheeze is clear. More people know of that; and more they know of
Sherman's treason in 1862, the better.[9] Came on interesting clippings of 1878 re/ my grand dad trying to get rider onto silver remonitization bill, that wd/ at least keep SOME of the non= interest=bearing debt in circulation as money.[1] Here's how. Hope
to git over in the spring.

[No closing]

1. Eduard Benes (1884-1948) had been president of Czechoslovakia (1935-38), but had resigned in protest over the German occupation of the Sudetenland. He headed the Czech government-in-exile from London (1940-45), promoting Czech independence during the war ("Benes"). Tafari (1892-1975) was Haile Selassie, Emperor of Ethiopia (1930-74), who headed the government-in-exile during the Italian occupation (1936-41) ("Haile Selassie"). Pound's reference to Hull's diplomacy is probably to suggest that, unlike Germany and Italy in their respective spheres of influence, American hegemony was experiencing no resistance in Latin America. Within a week of this letter, Hull was to bring off "a brilliant coup at the Havana Conference...by wangling conference approval of his

program for opposing transfer of European possessions in the New World" – a threatening prospect in light of recent German successes in Europe (Burns 436).

2. The "sheeny" refers to Secretary of the Treasury Morgenthau, whose report on gold purchases Pound had requested of Tinkham in his letter of 18 April (see Letter 92). Later in this letter Pound calls him "Morgenthaustein."

3. I have found no information on "Payne." For note on Grace Hamelin see Letter 88, n2.

4. For notes on D. R. Dewey and Thomas Dewey, see Letter 90, n1, and Letter 38, n2.

5. Ellery Sedgwick had been editor of *The Atlantic Monthly* for 30 years, leaving in 1938. Arthur Pound was Sedgwick's successor. Wendell Willkie (1892-1944) was the Republican presidential nominee in 1940. His pro-business and, especially, pro-utilities views were consistent with those of Arthur Pound, who, in addition to being the new editor and frequent contributor to the magazine, was also a noted economist, historian, and novelist ("Dr. Arthur Pound").

6. Henry Wallace was Roosevelt's running mate in 1940. The "24 elders" refers to *The Protocols of the Elders of Zion*, a 19th century forgery that "proved" that the Jews were plotting to take over the world (Parkes 45-56).

7. Judging from his remarks recorded in the *Congressional Record*, Senator Wheeler had little, if anything, to say about monetary policy *per se*. In a broader sense, however, he was a proponent of what he called "Economic Democracy" (not to be confused with Major Douglas' book by that name), which meant public rather than private ownership of natural resources and utilities ("Wheeler," *Current Biog.*).

8. Pound's article on the gold purchases may have been either "Gold Brokers," published in *Action*, 8 April 1939; or "Ezra Pound on Gold, War, and National Money," which is the *Capitol Daily* article of 9 May 1939, mentioned in Letter 81, n14 (Gallup, C1506, C1509).

9. Cf. Letters 90 and 91.

10. In "A Visiting Card," written two years later, Pound says he came upon these clippings in 1937. This letter indicates that he actually found them in 1940. In any case, his point is that his grandfather had been advocating "the same essentials of monetary and statal economics" that he himself has been writing about ("A Visiting Card" 325).

96. Pound to Tinkham

Via Marsala I2/5 Rapallo 28 Aug I940

Dear Unkle George
                    There bein no known deputato Denga or Tenka
/ and judgin from the internal evidence of the communication
I reckon the radio was onto you yester morn.[1]

Remeditatin on yrs of whenever May 24 and last to reach me
from
you/ strikes me that the time wd/now be timely for duputato
M/C and/or Senator to rise and suggest that henceforth the
Treasury KEEP and have for ready reference a LIST of
persons from whom they buy gold/ itemized/ and in case of
known and suspected crooks, that the said bastids be required
to say WHERE they got it/ and whether it had been passed thru
a string of N.Y. agents during the past 24 hours, or days.

Of course YOU and Hamilton and Vandebug[2] MAY have been
sellin it
to the govt. fer all I know, but unless you got a terrapin farm
(and/or aviary) or some other concealed asset beyond the figger
of my cal'lations, you cant (not even the three of you) have
sold 'em ALL ten billyum.

Of course IF the administration shd/ enlighten to point of puttin
me in charge (which they WONT) of the Treasury I wd/ cease
purchasin the d/n stuff altogether and lay in a stock of zinc or
some useful commodity.

                    SECOND/as Rip van Wendle seems to be wakin from
his
20 year sleep/ cd/ you suggest to him with my compliments that
he
lay off tellin the world what he dont know about europe under
impression that he knows it.   OR in parliamentary language,
that he
needn't accept my opinions (good as they doubtless are) but that
he
might exercise caution in accepting unverified information re/
YOURUP. with my comps/ and that I hope to call on him the
spring time at the residence round the corner from Buddha's
head.

with my compliments.

yrz deevotedly

I mean if Rip van W.W. is lookin forward/all he needs for campaign
purposes is mind our own business/if he gets in there will be
time for him to think about the etceteras.

1. "Denga" or "Tenka" was probably the Italian news reporter's mispronunciation of "Tinkham."
2. The references are to J. D. M. Hamilton, the Republican National Chair, and Arthur Hendrick Vandenberg, the Senator from Michigan.

97. Pound to Tinkham

[via Siberia, Japan, Giappone]

I2 Sept [1940]

Dear Miss Hamelin
          This is to say that mail via Japan Siberia takes
about a month and is NOT censored by the britisch at
Bermudah.

I dont know whether Mr Tinkham has sent me anything since
May 24.
That was the date of the last that has arrived (containing
treasury
letters)

                    since then
If he has written me anything I wish you cd/ find time to send
me copies via Japan/
I shd/ like any news possible.   Whether the acquisition of bases
in
Bermudah is *planned* to be ineffective against censorship/ i:e:
that all European news NOT controlled by Reuter, Havas etc/[1]
was
to be kept OUT at least until too late to be useful...

I shd/ also like a line on Willkie/ as seen by G.H.T.
The little news I get looks as if W/ was waking from long
sleep.

I wish he cd/ be persuaded NOT to believe any European news,
esp/
Reuter and Havas; in fact ANYTHING he had taken for
granted
about Europe during the past 2O years/
                    UNTIL he has had it
verified.

          cordiali saluti.

---

1. Reuters and Havas were the British and French news agencies. The
"acquisition of bases" refers to the British-American deal whereby British
military bases in Bermuda and Newfoundland were leased to the United States

"as an outright gift," and other British bases in the Americas were traded to the United States for fifty reconditioned destroyers (Burns 437-41). Though he does not mention it in his letters to Pound, Tinkham considered the destroyer deal treasonous ("Two Out" 21).

98. Tinkham to Pound

October 25, 1940

My dear Mr. Pound:

Your letter of September 12, "via Siberia, Japan, Giappone", has been received in the absence of Congressman Tinkham. He is now in the mountains of Virginia (Hot Springs) for a brief respite. His mail is not being forwarded to him. Your letter will be placed before him as soon as he returns to Washington, which I understand will be the day before the election on November 5, on his way to Boston.

It is my understanding that arrangements are being made for the acquisition of a base in Bermuda, as well as for the acquisition of other bases on islands northeast of the United States and in the Caribbean.

In the same mail with your letter there was received an envelope from Hot Springs containing, among other things, a copy of a communication which Congressman Tinkham wrote on October 22 to a close friend of his in Boston. In that letter he had the following to say about Willkie's chances for election:

"So far as the compaign is concerned, let me state the following facts for what they are worth. Mr. Roosevelt during the last eight years has raided the Treasury of twenty-five billions of dollars and most of this money has been expended under political direction. If those who have been bought stay bought, Willkie does not have a chance.

The question is, will they? My reports from New York State are uniformly good. Willkie must have New York State, and even with it he could lose. His chances seem to be improving, which may only mean, however, that the election will be close.

Johnson has helped in California, and I understand Lewis is coming out for Willkie, which will help in Pennsylvania and West Virginia particularly. Superficially, it looks like Roosevelt, but underneath, with the third-term issue and the question of war and peace, which Mr. Willkie has exploited slightly (agreeing with Roosevelt on foreign policy may have explosive force), we do not know. The Irish-American vote is going to be very important, particularly in Massachusetts, Rhode Island, Connecticut and New York, and there is some evidence that it is veering away from the radical elements.

"When the election is over we shall know more about the American people than we have ever known; perhaps we are too pessimistic. We shall have our answer then."

Mr. Tinkham has been much concerned over the position
taken by Mr. Willkie in relation to foreign affairs but I have heard him express the hope that he can be made "to see the light".
I have also heard him say repeatedly that he believed Mr. Willkie
to be "intellectually honest" and to possess "distinct ability".

Mr. Tinkham has taken the communications which you wrote
him earlier this year to his apartment. According to my office records, his last letter to you was the one you mentioned in your communication, dated May 24, 1940.

Sincerely yours,
[signed] G.C. Hamelin
Secretary to Mr. Tinkham

99. Pound to Tinkham

Via Marsala I2/5 Rapallo 7 Nov. I940

Dear Unkle George: Badly want some paper or report that will let
[me] guage the election. Especially want to know if you, Wheeler
and Bridges are still in (if they were up for election and you
haven't giv way to that wild fantasy for retirement that you
sprung
on me last year).[1] Rip van Wendle, despite boom and learning a
little, WAS 20 years behind the times. My first impression was
from lousy article reprint from Atlantic Monthly //Sedgwick
smear
WONT go down.[2]
Pennsylvania, aptly summarized in italia report by simple
parenthesis (Pittsburg Harrisburg) and the Conn/ dem/
congmen, must
be a joke on Sam Pryor?[3] or do I err?
        Vandenberg, as you said, is able/ BUT anchored, petrified
in dead wheezes, that ALL the rest of the world is onto. Japan
relations Manchuria, central China; Australia/Brazil.... all
ONTO
the old wheezes. Bridges wd/have been my pick as you weren't
running. BUT they ALL read the same damn papers. Worst of
the war
is the interruption of ANY proper communications service.
quite
needlessly as both sides wd/have let American ships pass. If
tackled proper way. Wasn't there a french loan to Manchuria a
while back when others were boycotting Manchu? Or is my
memory
twisted?

I packed up at beginning of Oct. to come home, but in Rome
found
NO clipper places till Dec. I5. (that wuz NO use if I was to find
out about the late elections... Nothing in europ press to show
Willkie wasn't kussing ALL Frankie's good deeds and backing
him up
in all his errors...however I had NO ADEQUATE data on which
to form an opinion...otherwise I might have got on the air, but
was afraid of doing more harm than good .... Anyhow prefer
Wallace to

McWhoosis...NO one will send me ANY news of Wallace stamp (i;e;
paper money) measures.[4]

As you may have noticed both Funk and Riccardi are now quoting me
without being aware of it .... or at any rate I am orthodox for
1940 instead of being a lone voice.[5] Believe this LITA air service
is all that works. They said Clipper so behind with mails that cd/
take no more passengers till Dec. 15...not that I necessarily
believe that yarn. Eddie Windsor headin for the ole Baltimore
boarding house.

Did the republicans attack Morgenthau AT ALL? If not, they
damn well deserve a lickin'.
Last real american papers I saw were dated June and came via
Siberia.

I shd/ like to come over in the spring if you will kindly stop the
horsetillities and put on a proper boat service.

[No closing]

---

1. All three men – Tinkham, Wheeler, and Bridges – were "still in." While
Senator Bridges did not have to run for reelection in 1940, Representative
Tinkham and Senator Wheeler did. Tinkham won with 59% of the vote, and
Wheeler won with 79% (*Congressional Quarterly's Guide* 622, 948).
2. The article Pound refers to is probably Willkie's "Political Power," published
in the *Atlantic Monthly* in August 1937, while Ellery Sedgwick was still editor. In
his article, Willkie, unlike Pound, is clearly an apologist for the utilities
companies. I do not know what Pound means by "Sedgwick smear" (cf. Letter
95, n5).
3. For note on Sam Pryor see Letter 81, n4.
4. "McWhoosis" refers to Charles Linza McNary (1874-1944), the U. S. Senator
from Oregon (1917-44) who was Willkie's running mate in 1940 ("McNary").
5. Walther Funk (1890-1960), a German journalist, economist, and former
Minister of Economics, was the Reichsbank president (1939-40). He would be
sentenced to life imprisonment for war crimes after the war. Raffaelo Riccardi
was the Italian Minister of Trade and Exchange from 1939. With Funk, he
planned for a post-war European economy that would be corporate and
autocratic. In this economy, national working power, by providing the backing
for the mark and the lire, would stabilize the currency, thereby relegating gold to
the periphery of the system ("Axis Pushes Plans"; "Reich Acts to Buoy Mark").
Commenting in the Fascist press, Riccardi declared there would be "no pity for
gold, which was used by the plutocratic nations as a means of political
enslavement of the poorer countries...gold will cease to be the arbiter of the
policy and economy and of the very existence of nations" ("Rome Gives

Design"). This conception of the post-war economy, along with its rationale, was consistent with Pound's way of thinking.

100. Pound to Tinkham

26 Dec. [1940]

And a Happy Xmas
Dear Unkle George
                    Waaaal they say the peepul votes AGAINST not
for
and they voted against the Atlantic Monthly; thank god and I
hope
they always will.[1]
Willkie's ignorance of europe equal to Ickes' / and brain??
even looser than I thought from original articles by him fed to
me
in N.Y.

NOT one mention of the defects of the administration/ at least
not
in all the stuff that has reached me up to now. Roosevelt played
all round in the field of verbal manifestation/ quite apart [from]
any funds employed.

Big Business (and Willkie is it) is the damnedest ass on earth/
still thinks a rotten monetary system is GOOD for business/ and
that a decent system is bad for business/despite ALL history,
from Pa colony before 1750/ on thru.

Waaal Europe has pretty well taken on the monetary ideas I
have
before now mentioned/

as to politics/ if you see the sacred S. Pryor[2]: repeat to him my
conviction that when the public is TIRED of something, you can
ONLY beat it by something DIFFERENT, not a weak
immitation.

Willkie in photo is a cross between Franklin D. and Bro/ Lower
the false alarm parson of Wyncote, Pa. as was in 1900.[3]

I still think the reps/ had ONCE chance of winning the election
     and they scrupulously omitted taking it. Do we place a
tomb stone on the party or wait for the second advent?

          yers

Can I have a congressional directory when the new ones come out?

1. The *Atlantic Monthly* was a supporter of Willkie. Cf. Letters 95 and 99.
2. For note on Sam Pryor see Letter 81, n4.
3. Rev. William Barnes Lower, who had become minister of the Calvary Presbyterian Church in Pound's childhood hometown of Wyncote, Pennsylvania, had lived with the Pound family for about 10 months in 1901-02. A writer of poetry himself, Rev. Lower may have influenced Pound's early interest in poetry, even though Pound did not especially admire him as a minister (Stock, *Pennsylvania* 14).

APPENDIX A: INDEX

This index includes the names of all persons referred to in the Pound/Tinkham correspondence and the letter-numbers of the letters in which the references appear. Where the persons are referred to by epithet or in some idiosyncratic way, I have included the reference itself in parentheses. If a person is referred to in both normal and unusual fashion in the same letter, I have preceded the idiosyncratic reference by the symbol "&"; for example, since Pound refers to Benito Mussolini in Letter 16 as "Mussolini" and as "Boss," I have indicated this dual reference as follows: 16 (& Boss).

Cross, Wilbur L., 58
Cutting, Bronson, 12

Daladier, Eduard, 16, 18, 41, 42, 43
Damrosch, Walter Johannes, 58, 91
Decatur, Stephen, 88
Delaisi, Francis, 10, 18, 28
Denga, 96
Dessari, 12
De Stefani, Alberto, 40
Dewey, Davis Rich, 90, 95
Dewey, Thomas Edmund, 38, 89
    (Vandendewey), 95 (Tommy)
Douglas, Clifford Hugh, 8, 15, 16, 32,
    35 (Doug), 43 (Doug), 54 (expert
    advisor), 59, 81
Duboin, 16, 28
Dunn, J. W. G., Jr., 43, 49
Dupont (family), 29, 53

Eccles, Marrimer Stoddard, 29
Eden, Robert Anthony, 12 (& Master
    Tony, Tony E.), 14, 18, 35, 56, 81
Edison, Thomas Alva, 59
Edward VIII, 35 (Ed), 40 (Edward to-
    be Simpson), 42, 43 (Eddie), 99
    (Eddie Windsor)
Egan, Maurice Francis, 58
Eliot, T. S., 33, 56
Erigena, Scotus, 81

Fack, Hugo, 15
Farinacci, Roberto, 15
Farley, James Aloysius, 45
Ford, Henry, 16, 30, 31, 54
Ford, Thomas Francis, 57
Franco, Francisco, 42
Frankfurter, Felix, 8, 30
Franklin, Benjamin, 18
Frazier, Lynn J., 35
Fuller, John Frederick Charles, 44, 63
Funk, Walther, 99

Garner, John Nance (Jack), 82, 89
George VI, 35
Gesell, Silvio, 41, 43
Gilbert, Cass, 58
Goldsborough, Thomas Alan, 59
Grant, Robert, 58
Grant, Ulysses S., 34, 88

Gregory, Theodore Emanuel
    Guggenheim, 60 (Gregories)
Grey, James C., 74
Grigg, Edward, 82
Guggenheim (family), 60

Hadley, Arthur Twining, 58
Haile Selassi. See Tafari
Hamilton, Alexander, 16, 38
Hamilton, John David Miller, 29, 30,
    96
Hamelin, Grace C., 88 (Miss H.), 95
Harding, Warren G., 38
Harmsworth, Harold Sidney, see
    Rothermere
Hawk, Harold W., 34
Hayes, Rutherford Birchard, 90
Hearst, William Randolph, 53 (Hirst)
Herter, Christian Archibald, 74
Hitler, Adolph, 16, 40, 41, 42, 44
    (Fuhrer), 60, 81
Hoare, Samuel John Gurney, 35
Hollis, Christopher, 15, 16, 20, 44
Hoover, Herbert Clark, 10, 16, 29, 30
House, Edward Mandel, 29
Howells, William Dean, 58
Huddleston, Sisley, 43
Hull, Cordell, 18, 43, 95

Ibbotson, Joseph Darling (Bib), 55
Ickes, Harold LeClaire, 30 (Ikevitch),
    100
Isaacsohn, 30

Jackson, Andrew, 16, 27
James, Henry, 55
Jefferson, Thomas, 15, 18 (Jeff), 45,
    53, 55
Johnson, Andrew, 65
Johnson, Hewlett, 42 (& Dean)
Joyce, James, 90

Kennedy, Joseph Patrick, 59
Keynes, John Maynard, 15 (& K/), 16
    (a man who is READ by govt.
    economists), 60, 65
Kimball, Dexter, 8
Kitasono, Katue, 41, 54
Knitel, 41, 42 (Bloke from Cairo)
Knox, Frank, 94 (idiot)

APPENDIX B: LIST OF PERSONS MENTIONED IN POUND'S LETTERS TO TINKHAM AND *THE CANTOS*.

This list includes the names of all persons that Pound mentions in both his letters to Tinkham and *The Cantos*. The numbers are Canto numbers. Where Pound refers to a person by some other name in *The Cantos*, I have supplied his actual mode of reference parenthetically. For example, in Canto 22 he refers to John Maynard Keynes as "BUKOS," so in the list the Keynes entry is as follows: Keynes, John Maynard, 22 (BUKOS). In compiling the list I consulted Edwards and Vasse's *Annotated Index to the Cantos of Ezra Pound* and Carroll F. Terrell's *A Companion to the Cantos of Ezra Pound*, both of which are included in the bibliography at the end of this volume.

Adams Brooks, 97

Adams, John, 31, 32, 33, 37, 48, 50, 52, 62, 63, 64, 65, 66, 67, 68, 69, 70, 71, 74, 76, 81, 84, 88, 89, 94, 95, 97, 100

Agresti, Olivia Rossetti, 76

Asquith, Herbert Henry, 77

Bacon, Francis S., 12 (Baldy)

Bankhead, John Hollis, 84

Biddle, Nicholas, 34, 37, 88, 89, 94, 103

Blum, Leon, 80

Borah, William Edgar, 84, 89

Bottai, Giuseppe, 92

Bunting, Basil, 74, 110

Cato, 86

Confucius (or Kung), 13, 52, 53, 54, 55, 56, 57, 58, 59, 60, 61, 67, 76, 77, 80

Douglas, (Major) Clifford Hugh, 22, 38, 41, 46, 87, 97, 100

Edward VIII (Windsor), 74, 80, 89, 95, 100, 109

Eliot, Thomas Stearns (T. S.)., 46, 65, 74 (Possum), 77, 80, 81 (Possum), 98 (Possum), 102 (Possum)

Erigena, Scotus, 36, 74, 83, 85, 87, 88, 90, 92, 100, 105, 109

Farley, James Aloysius, 46

Ford, Henry, 74

Franco, Francisco, 81

Franklin, Benjamin, 31, 33, 34, 52, 62, 63, 64, 65, 67, 68, 69, 71

Gesell, Silvio., 74, 80

Gregory, Theodore Emanual Guggenheim, 52

Hamilton, Alexander, 37, 62, 63, 66, 69, 70, 71, 88, 89

Hayes, Rutherford Birchard, 76

Hitler, Adolph, 62, 74 (H.), 76 (Fuhrer), 104

Hollis, Christopher, 104

Howells, William Dean, 104

Jackson, Andrew, 34, 37, 80, 88, 89, 100

James, Henry, 7 (great domed head), 12, 74, 79

BIBLIOGRAPHY

"$10,000,000 for Peace New Carnegie Gift." *New York Times* 15 Dec. 1910, late ed.: 1-2.

"Adams, Samuel Hopkins." *Oxford Companion to American Literature*, 1965 ed.

"Alberta Delays Budget." *New York Times* 28 Mar. 1937, late ed.: 4.

"Alberta is Swept by Social Credit." *New York Times* 23 Aug. 1935, late ed.: 9.

"Allows Mission to Spain." *New York Times* 30 Mar. 1937, late ed.: 4.

"Altrincham Dies; British Lord, 76." *New York Times* 2 Dec. 1955, late ed.: 27.

"Angell, Sir Norman." *Webster's New Biographical Dictionary*. 1983 ed.

"Anglo-U. S. Treaty on Trade Nearer." *New York Times* 26 Jan. 1937, late ed.: 6.

"Angus Would Set Up $10,000,000,000 Fund." *New York Times* 22 Feb. 1938, late ed.: 32.

"Arthur Raffalovich." *New York Times* 13 Jan. 1922, late ed.: 14.

"Astor, Waldorf." *Dictionary of National Biography, 1951-1960.* 1971 ed.

"Attacks on Sir O. Mosley." *The Times* (London) 6 Nov. 1939, Royal ed.: 3.

Auslander, Joseph. "Words." *Sunrise Trumpets.* New York: Harper, 1924. 1.

"Auslander, Joseph." *Oxford Companion to American Literature.* 1965 ed.

"Axis Pushes Plans for Post-War Europe." *New York Times* 22 Oct. 1940, late ed.: 4.

"Backs Retail Discount." *New York Times* 1 Mar. 1938, late ed.: 38.

"Baldwin, Stanley." *Webster's New Biographical Dictionary.* 1983 ed.

"Bankhead, John Hollis." *Biographical Directory of the American Congress 1774-1971.* 1977 ed.

"Bankhead, William Brockman." *Biographical Directory of the American Congress 1774-1971.* 1971 ed.

"Baruch, Bernard Mannes." *Webster's New Biographical Dictionary.* 1983 ed.

"Beat French Red Deputy." *New York Times* 27 July 1936, late ed.: 4.

"Benes, Eduard." *Webster's New Biographical Dictionary.* 1983 ed.

"Blum, Leon." *Webster's New Biographical Dictionary.* 1983 ed.

"Bonnet, Georges-Etienne." *Webster's New Biographical Dictionary.* 1983 ed.

Bradley, Francine. Letter. *New York Times* 17 Apr. 1935, late ed.: 22.

"Bridges, Henry Styles." *Biographical Directory of the American Congress 1774-1971.* 1971 ed.

"Britain is Seeking Talks with Gandhi." *New York Times* 9 Apr. 1937, late ed.: 16.

"British Bank Head Hits U. S. on Silver." *New York Times* 30 Jan. 1936, late ed.: 27, 34.

"British Treaty with Poland." *The Times* (London) 20 Oct. 1939, Royal ed.: 3.

Brockway, Archibald Fenner. *The Bloody Traffic.* London: Gollancz, 1933.

Burns, James MacGregor. *Roosevelt: The Lion and the Fox.* New York: Harcourt, 1956.

"Butler, Nicholas Murray." *Webster's New Biographical Dictionary.* 1983 ed.

"Canada Plans Rule Over Arms-Making." *New York Times* 1 Apr. 1937, late ed.: 9.

"Canada Studying Ban on War Profit." *New York Times* 3 Apr. 1937, late ed.: 9.

Cannistraro, Philip V. "Rossoni, Edmondo." *Historical Dictionary of Fascist Italy.* Westport, CT: Greenwood P, 1982.

_____. "Spirito, Ugo." *Historical Dictionary of Fascist Italy.* Westport, CT: Greenwood P, 1982.

Canterbury, John B. " 'Ham and Eggs' in California." *Nation* 147 (1938): 408-10.

"Carleton, Mark Alfred." *New Century Cyclopedia of Names.* 1954 ed.

Carroll, Howard. "Third Generation Rules Mellon Clan." *New York Times* 6 Sep. 1937, late ed.: 10.

"Cato, Marcus Porcius." *Webster's New Biographical Dictionary.* 1983 ed.

"Cecil, Robert Arthur James Gascoyne." *Webster's New Biographical Dictionary.* 1983 ed.

"Chamberiain, Neville." *Webster's New Biographical Dictionary.* 1983 ed.

Clark, William Bedford. "'ez sez': pound's 'pithy promulgations.' " *Antioch Review* 37 (1979): 420-27.

"Cohen, Benjamin Victor." *New Century Cyclopedia of Names.* 1954 ed.

Comay, Joan. *Who's Who in Jewish History after the Period of the Old Testament.* London: Weidenfeld, 1974.

"Company Meetings: Birmingham Small Arms Company." *The Times* (London) 13 Nov. 1935. Royal ed.: 19.

"Company Meetings: Westminster Bank." *The Times* (London) 30 Jan. 1936, Royal ed.: 22.

Congress and the Nation 1945-1964: A Review of Government and Politics in the Postwar Years. Washington: Congressional Quarterly Service, 1965.

Congressional Quarterly's Guide to U. S. Elections. 2nd ed. Washington: Congressional Quarterly, 1985.

Cong. Rec. 3 Feb. 1933: 3336-39.

_____. 11 Mar. 1933: 89, 195.

_____. 30 Mar. 1933: 1027-35.

_____. 13 Apr. 1933: 1625.

_____. 14 May 1935: 7526-34.

_____. 14 Jan. 1937: 226.

_____. 24 Feb. 1937: 1563-64, 1571.

_____. 9 Apr. 1937: 3313.

_____. 25 May 1937: 5043.

_____. 8 June 1937: 5438.

_____. 24 Nov. 1937: 362.

_____. 24 Jan. 1938: 1010.

_____. 23 Jan. 1939: 640.

_____. 15 May 1939: 5561.

_____. 4 Aug. 1939: 11, 117.

_____. 22 Jan. 1940, App.: 292.

Cortesi, Arnaldo. "Algerians Aiding in Spain, Rome Says." *New York Times* 15 Apr. 1937, late ed.: 4.

"Coughlin, Charles Edward." *Webster's New Biographical Dictionary.* 1983 ed.

Croft, Sir Henry Page. "Closing Suez Canal." *New York Times* 1 Sep. 1935, late ed., sec. 4: 8.

Cross, Colin. *The Fascists in Britain.* London: Barrie, 1961.

"Cross, Wilbur Lucius." *Webster's New Biographical Dictionary.* 1983 ed.

Crowther, Samuel. "Only Real Security: An Interview with Henry Ford." *Saturday Evening Post* 1 Feb. 1936: 5-7.

_____. "Our Job: An Interview with Henry Ford." *Saturday Evening Post* 31 Oct. 1936: 5-7.

Cumulative Index of Congressional Committee Hearings 1935-1958. Westport, CT: Greenwood P, 1973.

Cutting, Bronson. Letter to Ezra Pound. 24 May 1934. The Yale Collection of American Literature, Beinecke Rare Book and Manuscript Library, Yale University.

"Daladier, Edvard." *Webster's New Biographical Dictionary*. 1983 ed.

"Damrosch, Walter Johannes." *New Century Cyclopedia of Names*. 1954 ed.

Davis, Earl. *Vision Fugitive: Ezra Pound and Economics*. Lawrence, KS: UP of Kansas, 1968.

Davis, John H. *The Guggenheims: An American Epic*. New York: William Morrow, 1978.

"Dean of Canterbury on Spiritual Forces." *The Times* (London) 19 Apr. 1937, Royal ed.: 16.

"Decatur, Stephen." *Webster's American Biographies*. 1974 ed.

DeGrand, Alexander J. "Bottai, Giuseppe." *Dictionary of Modern Italian History*. Westport, CT: Greenwood P, 1985.

"Farinacci, Roberto." *Dictionary of Modern Italian History*. Westport, CT: Greenwood P, 1985.

"Volpi, Guiseppe." *Dictionary of Modern Italian History*. Westport, CT: Greenwood P, 1985.

Devendittis, Paul J. "Corriere Della Sera." *Dictionary of Modern Italian History*. Westport, CT: Greenwood P, 1985.

"Dewey, Davis Rich." *New Century Cyclopedia of Names*. 1954 ed.

"Dewey, Thomas Edward." *Webster's New Biographical Dictionary*. 1983 ed.

Dillard, Dudley. "Keynesian Economics." *Encyclopedia of Economics*. Ed. Douglas Greenwald. New York: McGraw, 1982. 571-77.

"Douglas, Clifford Hugh." *Webster's New Biographical Dictionary*. 1983 ed.

"Dr. Arthur Pound, Historian, is Dead." *New York Times* 15 Jan. 1966, late ed.: 27.

"Dr. T. Spencer, 45, Long at Harvard." *New York Times* 19 Jan. 1949, late ed.: 27.

"Eccles, Marrimer Stoddard." *Webster's New Biographical Dictionary*. 1983 ed.

"Eden, Anthony." *New Century Cyclopedia of Names*. 1954 ed.

Edgett, Edwin Francis. "Liveright, Horace Brisbin." *Dictionary of American Biography*. Supplement One. 1944 ed.

Edwards, John Hamilton, and William W. Vasse. *Annotated Index to the Cantos of Ezra Pound: Cantos I-LXXXIV*. Berkeley: U of California P, 1971.

Elliott, David R. "Aberhart, William." *The Canadian Encyclopedia*. 1985 ed.

"Erigina, Scotus." *Webster's New Biographical Dictionary*. 1983 ed.

"Farley, James Aloysius." *Webster's New Biographical Dictionary*. 1983 ed.

Finlay, John L. *Social Credit: The English Origins*. Montreal: McGill-Queen's UP, 1972.

"Ford, Thomas Francis." *Biographical Directory of the American Congress 1774-1971*. 1971 ed.

"Foreign Loan Plan is Denied in Berlin." *New York Times* 2 Sep. 1935, late ed.: 21.

"Frankfurter, Felix." *Webster's New Biographical Dictionary*. 1983 ed.

"Frazier, Lynn J." *Biographical Directory of the American Congress 1774-1971.* 1971 ed.

"Fuhrer at German Motor Show: The Mark and Production." *The Times* (London) 19 Feb. 1938, Royal ed.: 11.

Gallup, Donald. *Ezra Pound: A Bibliography.* Charlottesville: UP of Virginia, 1983.

"Garner, John Nance." *Webster's New Biographical Dictionary.* 1983 ed.

Gefin, Laszlo K. *Ideogram: History of a Poetic Method.* Austin: U of Texas P, 1982.

"George V's Cousin, 45, Dies in London." *New York Times* 9 Apr. 1938, late ed.: 17.

"Gervase Beckett, English Banker." *New York Times* 25 Aug. 1937, late ed.: 21.

"Goldsborough, Thomas Alan." *Biographical Directory of the American Congress 1774-1971.* 1971 ed.

Gore, John. "Wigram, Clive." *Dictionary of National Biography 1951-1960.* 1971 ed.

"Guns." *Newsweek* 15 Feb. 1936: 7-11.

"Haile Selassie." *Webster's New Biographical Dictionary.* 1983 ed.

Haines, C. Crove, and Ross J. S. Hoffman. *The Origins and Background of the Second World War.* New York: Oxford UP, 1947.

Harlow, Alvin F. "Straus, Jesse Isidor." *Dictionary of American Biography.* Supplement Two. 1958 ed.

"Harmsworth, Harold Sidney." *New Century Cyclopedia of Names.* 1954 ed.

Hawk, Harold W. Letter to Ezra Pound. 15 Feb. 1936. The Yale Collection of American Literature, Beinecke Rare Book and Manuscript Library, Yale University.

_____. Letter to Ezra Pound. 3 May 1936. The Yale Collection of American Literature, Beinecke Rare Book and Manuscript Library, Yale University.

Heymann, C. David. *Ezra Pound: The Last Rower.* New York: Viking, 1976.

"House, Edward Mandell." *Webster's New Biographical Dictionary.* 1983 ed.

"House Gets Report on Neutrality Bill." *New York Times* 29 Jan. 1936, late ed.: 4.

"Huddleston, Sisley." *New Century Cyclopedia of Names.* 1954 ed.

"Ickes, Harold LeClaire." *Webster's New Biographical Dictionary.* 1983 ed.

"Italian Ex-Finance Chief Becomes Advisor to China." *New York Times* 5 Mar. 1937, late ed.: 9.

Jackson, Gabriel. *The Spanish Republic and the Civil War 1931-1939.* Princeton: Princeton UP, 1965.

Jackson, Julian. *The Politics of Depression in France 1932-1936.* Cambridge: Cambridge UP, 1985.

"James C. Grey." *New York Times* 26 Sep. 1943, late ed.: 48.

"Jerzy Potocki, 72, Diplomat, is Dead." *New York Times* 22 Sep. 1961, late ed.: 34.

Johnson, Hewlett. Letter. *The Times* (London) 5 May 1937, Royal ed.: 12.

Keleher, Edward P. "The Nazi-Soviet Pact." *Great Events from History.* Ed. Frank N. Magill. Vol. 3 of Modern European Series. Englewood Cliffs, NJ: Salem P, 1973. 1433-36.

Kelly, Alfred H., and Winfred A. Harbison. *The American Constitution: Its Origins and Development.* New York: Norton, 1948.

"Kennedy, Joseph Patrick." *Webster's New Biographical Dictionary.* 1983 ed.

Kimpel, Ben D., and T. C. Duncan Eaves. " 'Tremaine at 2 in the Morning' Other Little Mysteries." *Paideuma* 10 (1981): 307-10.

Klinck, Dennis R. "Pound's 'economist consulted of nations.' " *Paideuma* 5 (1976): 67-68.

Krock, Arthur. "How a 'Coalition' Can Manage Defense by Existing Law." *New York Times* 21 May 1940, late ed.: 22.

"Krutch, Joseph Wood." *New Century Cyclopedia of Names*. 1954 ed.

Kuhn, Ferdinand, Jr. "Trade Pact is Held Sole Runciman Aim." *New York Times* 18 Jan. 1937, late ed.: 8.

"Lady Sieff Dies: Zionist Leader, 75." *New York Times* 9 Jan. 1966, late ed.: 56.

"LaFollette, Robert Marion, Jr." *Biographical Directory of the American Congress 1774-1971*. 1971 ed.

"Landon, Alfred Mossman." *Webster's New Biographical Dictionary*. 1983 ed.

"Lang, Cosmo Gordon." *Webster's New Biographical Dictionary*. 1983 ed.

"Larkins Buy Store in Chicago." *New York Times* 6 Sep. 1925, late ed. , sec. 2: 2.

Larmour, Peter J. *The French Radical Party in the 1930s*. Stanford: Stanford UP, 1964.

Lasswell, Harold D. "The Study and Practice of Propaganda." *Propaganda and Promotional Activities, an Annotated Bibliography*. By Lasswell, Ralph D. Casey, and Bruce Lannes. Chicago: U of Chicago P, 1969. 1-27.

Laughlin, James. *Pound as Wuz: Essays and Lectures on Ezra Pound*. Saint Paul: Graywolf P, 1987.

"Laval, Pierre." *Webster's New Biographical Dictionary*. 1983 ed.

"Learned Societies Elect." *New York Times* 31 Dec. 1936, late ed.: 4.

"Leigh, William Colston." *Current Biography*. 1942 ed.

"Lewis, James Hamilton." *Biographical Directory of the American Congress 1774-1971*. 1971 ed.

"Lewis, Percy Wyndham." *Webster's New Biographical Dictionary*. 1983 ed.

"Lindbergh, Charles A(ugustus)." *Current Biography*. 1941 ed.

"Lodge, Henry Cabot, Jr." *Biographical Directory of the American Congress 1774-1971*. 1971 ed.

MacCormac, John. "Social Credit Plan Faces Uncertainty." *New York Times* 14 Mar. 1937, late ed., sec. 1: 6.

"MacDonald, James Ramsay." *Webster's New Biographical Dictionary*. 1983 ed.

Makin, Peter. *Provence and Pound*. Berkeley: U of California P, 1978.

"Many Years at Harvard: Prof. Sprague Went to Bank of England in 1930." *New York Times* 24 May 1933, late ed.: 3.

"Mark Sullivan, 77, Columnist, is Dead." *New York Times* 15 Aug. 1952, late ed.: 15.

"Marks & Spenser Ltd." *Moody's International Manual*. 1981 ed.

"Martin, Joseph William, Jr." *Biographical Directory of the American Congress 1774-1971*. 1971 ed.

Materer, Timothy. Commentary. *Pound/Lewis: The Letters of Ezra Pound and Wyndham Lewis*. Ed. Materer. New York: New Directions, 1985.

Mazgaj, Paul. *The Action Française and Revolutionary Syndicalism*. Chapel Hill: U of North Carolina P, 1979.

McKee, Oliver, Jr. "Tinkham." *North American Review* 230 (1930): 297-304.

"McNary, Charles Linza." *Biographical Directory of the American Congress 1774-1971*. 1971 ed.

"Mellon, Andrew William." *New Century Cyclopedia of Names*. 1954 ed.

"Mencken, Henry Lewis." *Webster's New Biographical Dictionary*. 1983 ed.

"Mensdorff-Pouilly-Dietrichstein, Count Albert von." *New Century Cyclopedia of Names*. 1954 ed.

Miller, John C. *Alexander Hamilton: Portrait in Paradox*. New York: Harper, 1959.

"Mills, Ogden Livingston." *New Century Cyclopedia of Names*. 1954 ed.

"Molotov, Vyacheslav Mikhailovich." *New Century Cyclopedia of Names*. 1954 ed.

"Montagu Norman Arrives in Canada for 'Holiday' " *New York Times* 11 Aug. 1935, late ed., sec. 3: 7.

"Montagu Norman Sails." *New York Times* 7 Sep. 1935, late ed.: 8.

"Morgenthau, Henry." *Webster's New Biographical Dictionary*. 1983 ed.

"Morgenthau, Henry, Jr." *Webster's New Biographical Dictionary*. 1983 ed.

"Mosley, Sir Oswald Ernald." *Webster's New Biographical Dictionary*. 1983 ed.

"Mrs. Francis Tweddle." *New York Times* 23 Oct. 1955, late ed.: 86.

"Munson, Gorham B." *New Century Cyclopedia of Names*. 1954 ed.

National Party Conventions 1831-1980. Ed. Patricia M. Russotto. Washington: Congressional Quarterly, 1983.

"Nazi Election Crusade: Bread and Gold." *The Times* (London) 30 Mar. 1938, Royal ed.: 13.

"Necker, Jacques." *New Century Cyclopedia of Names*. 1954 ed.

"New Party Invites Vandenberg." *New York Times* 29 Sep. 1937, late ed.: 3.

Nicholls, Peter. *Ezra Pound: Politics, Economics and Writing*. London: Macmillan P, 1984.

"Nicolson, Harold." *Obituaries from the Times, 1961-1970*. Reading, Eng.: Newspaper Archives Development Service, 1975.

"Niemeyer Coming on Bond Mission." *New York Times* 17 Jan. 1937, late ed.: 28.

"Norman, Montagu Collet." *New Century Cyclopedia of Names*. 1954 ed.

"Nye. Gerald P." *New Century Cyclopedia of Names*. 1954 ed.

"Paish, Sir George." *Webster's New Biographical Dictionary*. 1983 ed.

Parkes, James. *Antisemitism*. Chicago: Quadrangle Books, 1963.

Patterson, James T. *Congressional Conservatism and the New Deal*. Lexington, KY: U of Kentucky P, 1967.

Pearce, Donald, and Herbert Schneidau. Glossary. *Ezra Pound/John Theobald Letters*. Ed. Pearce and Schneidau. Redding Ridge, CT: Black Swan Books, 1984. 156-61.

Pearlman, Daniel. "Fighting the World: The Letters of Ezra Pound to Senator William E. Borah of Idaho." *Paideuma* 12 (1983): 419-26.

"Peek, George Nelson." *Concise Dictionary of American Biography*. 1977 ed.

"People." *Time* 6 Sep. 1936: 72.

Perelman, Ch., and L. Olbrechts-Tyteca. *The New Rhetoric: A Treatise on Argumentation*. Trans. John Wilkinson and Purcell Weaver. Notre Dame, London: U of Notre Dame P, 1979.

"Perkins, Frances." *Webster's New Biographical Dictionary*. 1983 ed.

"Peruvian is on Way Here." *New York Times* 12 Nov. 1939, late ed., sec. 1: 31.

Philip, P. J. "France Ends Curb on Gold to Regain Vast Sum Abroad." *New York Times* 6 Mar. 1937, late ed.: 1.

Pilkington, Walter. Introduction. *Letters to Ibbotson, 1935-1952*. By Ezra Pound. Ed. Vittoria I. Mandolfo and Margaret Hurley. Orono, ME: National Poetry Foundation, 1979. 1-8.

"Pinchot, Amos Richards Eno." *Who's Who in America 1944-1945*. 1944 ed.

"Points in Molotoff Speech." *New York Times* 1 Nov. 1939, late ed.: 8.

Pound, Ezra Loomis. *America, Roosevelt and the Causes of the Present War.* London: Peter Russell, 1951.

_____. "American Notes." *New English Weekly* 6 (1935): 270.

_____. "American Notes." *New English Weekly* 7 (1935): 185.

_____. "American Notes." *New English Weekly* 7 (1935): 205.

_____. "American Notes." *New English Weekly* 7 (1935): 225-26.

_____. "American Notes." *New English Weekly* 8 (1936): 265.

_____. "American Notes." *New English Weekly* 8 (1936): 465.

_____. "Books and Music." *"Ezra Pound Speaking": Radio Speeches of World War II.* Ed. Leonard W. Doob. Contributions in American Studies 37. Westport, CT: Greenwood P, 1978. 7-10.

_____. "Bravo Roosevelt!" *New English Weekly* 10 (1936): 187.

_____. "The Cabinet of a Dream, and Congress Should Go on the Air." *Greenwich Time* 13 July 1939: 4.

_____. *Cantos LII-LXXI.* London: Faber, 1940.

_____. *The Cantos of Ezra Pound.* New York: New Directions, 1972.

_____. "Current Hopes and Leftover Blind Spots." *New Democracy* 1 (1934): 4.

_____. "Ecclesiastical History." *New English Weekly* 5 (1934): 272-73.

_____. "Gold and Work." *Selected Prose 1909-1965.* Ed. William Cookson. New York: New Directions, 1973. 336-351.

_____. *Guide to Kulchur.* New York: New Directions, 1970.

_____. "An Impact." *Impact: Essays On Ignorance and the Decline of American Civilization.* Chicago: Henry Regnery, 1960. 142-56.

_____. "Indecision." *"Ezra Pound Speaking": Radio Speeches of World War II.* Ed. Leonard W. Doob. Contributions in American Studies 37. Westport, CT: Greenwood P, 1978. 84-86.

_____. "An Introduction to the Economic Nature of the United States." *Selected Prose 1909-1965.* Ed. William Cookson. New York: New Directions, 1973. 167-85.

_____. "Introductory Textbook." *Selected Prose 1909-1965.* Ed. William Cookson. New York: New Directions, 1973. 159-60.

_____. "The Jefferson-Adams Correspondence." *North American Review* 244 (1937): 314-324.

_____. *Jefferson and/or Mussolini.* New York: Liveright. 1970.

_____. Letter to Franklin D. Roosevelt. 2 May 1933. The Yale Collection of American Literature, Beinecke Rare Book and Manuscript Library, Yale Univeristy.

_____. Letter to Franklin D. Roosevelt. 27 April 1934. The Yale Collection of American Literature, Beinecke Rare Book and Manuscript Library, Yale University.

_____. Letter to Henry Morgenthau, Sr. October 1934. The Yale Collection of American Literature, Beinecke Rare Book and Manuscript Library, Yale University.

_____. Letter to William E. Borah. 8 May 1934. The Yale Collection of American Literature, Beinecke Rare Book and Manuscript Library, Yale University.

_____. "More Homely." *"Ezra Pound Speaking": Radio Speeches of World War II.* Ed. Leonard W. Doob. Contributions in American Studies 37. Westport, CT: Greenwood P, 1978. 221-24.

_____. "Mr. Roosevelt at the Crossroads." *New Democracy* 2 (1934): 5.

————. "On Resuming." *"Ezra Pound Speaking": Radio Speeches of World War II*. Ed. Leonard W. Doob. Contributions in American Studies 37. Westport, CT: Greenwood P, 1978. 23-27.

————. "The Pattern." *"Ezra Pound Speaking": Radio Speeches of World War II*. Ed. Leonard W. Doob. Contributions in American Studies 37. Westport, CT: Greenwood P, 1978. 78-80.

————. "Peace." *Selected Prose 1909-1965*. Ed. William Cookson. New York: New Directions, 1973. 222-23.

————. "Points." *New Democracy* 1 (1933): 4.

————. "Pots to Fracture." *"Ezra Pound Speaking": Radio Speeches of World War II*. Ed. Leonard W. Doob. Contributions in American Studies 37. Westport, CT: Greenwood P, 1978. 240-43.

————. "Power." *"Ezra Pound Speaking": Radio Speeches of World War II*. Ed. Leonard W. Doob. Contributions in American Studies 37. Westport, CT: Greenwood P, 1978. 41-43.

————. "Race." *New English Weekly* 10 (1936): 12-13.

————. "Serviti." *"Ezra Pound Speaking": Radio Speeches of World War II*. Ed. Leonard W. Doob. Contributions in American Studies 37. Westport, CT: Greenwood P, 1978. 229-30.

————. "This Super Neutrality." *The New Age* 17 (1915): 595.

————. "To Recapitulate." *"Ezra Pound Speaking": Radio Speeches of World War II*. Ed. Leonard W. Doob. Contributions in American Studies 37. Westport, CT: Greenwood P, 1978. 259-61.

————. "To William Langer, Governor of North Dakota." *Impact: Essays on Ignorance and the Decline of American Civilizations*. Chicago: Henry Regnery, 1960. 273-74.

————. "A Visiting Card." *Selected Letters 1909-1915*. Ed. William Cookson. New York: New Directions, 1973. 306-35.

"Pound, Sir Dudley." *Webster's New Biographical Dictionary*. 1983 ed.

"Pound, Thaddeus Coleman." *Biographical Directory of the American Congress 1774-1971*. 1971 ed.

"Powers Sign Pact on Capitulations." *New York Times* 9 May 1937, late ed.: 22.

Read, Forrest. Commentary. *Pound/Joyce: The Letters of Ezra Pound to James Joyce*. Ed. Read. New York: New Directions, 1967.

Reck, Michael. *Ezra Pound: A Close-up*. London: Rupert Hart-Davis, 1968.

"Reich Acts to Buoy Mark in Balkans." *New York Times* 21 Oct. 1940, late ed.: 27.

"Republican Group Picks S. F. Pryor Jr." *New York Times* 18 May 1940, late ed.: 34.

"Ribbentrop, Joachim von." *New Century Cyclopedia of Names*. 1954 ed.

Ricardo, Nathan. "Rothschild." *The Universal Jewish Encyclopedia*. New York: The Universal Jewish Encyclopedia, 1943.

Rickett, Denis. "Salter, (James) Arthur." *Dictionary of National Biography 1971-1980*. 1986 ed.

"Rome Gives Design for New Economy." *New York Times* 11 Oct. 1940, late ed.: 4.

Roosevelt, Franklin D. *Looking Forward*. New York: John Day, 1933.

————. *The Public Papers and Addresses of Franklin D. Roosevelt*. 13 vols. New York: Random House, 1938. 2: 264-65.

"Roper, Daniel Calhoun." *New Century Cyclopedia of Names*. 1954 ed.

"Rota, Ettore." *Enciclopedia Italiana di Scienze, Lettere ed Arti 1938-1948.* Appendix II, III. Rome: Institute della Enciclopedia Italiana, 1949, 1961.

"Rupert E. Beckett." *New York Times* 26 Apr. 1955, late ed.: 29.

Salvemini, Gaetano. *The French Revolution, 1788-1792.* Trans. I. M. Rawson. New York: Norton, 1962.

"Sauerwein, Jules." *New Century Cyclopedia of Names.* 1954 ed.

"Schacht, Horace Greeley Hjalmar." *Webster's New Biographical Dictionary.* 1983 ed.

Schlesinger, Arthur M., Jr. "Sources of the New Deal." *The New Deal: What Was It?* Ed. Morton Keller. New York: Holt, 1963. 94-104.

"Sees U. S. Approaching War." *New York Times* 4 Nov. 1935, late ed.: 13.

Seldes, George. *Iron, Blood and Profits.* New York: Harper, 1934.

"Sieff, Israel Moses." *Obituaries from the Times, 1971-1975.* Westport, CT: Newspaper Archives Development, 1978.

Skidelsky, Robert. *Oswald Mosley.* New York: Holt, 1975.

"Skoda Works." *New Century Cyclopedia of Names.* 1954 ed.

"Smith, Alfred Emanuel." *New Century Cyclopedia of Names.* 1954 ed.

"Steed, Henry Wickham." *Chambers Biographical Dictionary.* 1974 ed.

"Steffens, Joseph Lincoln." *Webster's New Biographical Dictionary.* 1983 ed.

Sternsher, Bernard. *Rexford Tugwell and the New Deal.* New Brunswick, NJ: Rutgers UP, 1964.

Stock, Noel. *The Life of Ezra Pound.* New York: Random House, 1970.

_____. *Ezra Pound's Pennsylvania.* Toledo: The Friends of the University of Toledo Library, 1976.

Stoddard, Lothtop." *New Century Cyclopedia of Names.* 1954 ed.

"Stone, Harlan Fiske." *New Century Cyclopedia of Names.* 1954 ed.

"Streit, Clarence Kirshman." *New Century Cyclopedia of Names.* ed.

"Taft, Robert Alphonso." *New Century Cyclopedia of Names.* 1954 ed.

"Tannery, Jean." *New Century Cyclopedia of Names.* 1954 ed.

Terrell, Carroll F. *A Companion to the Cantos of Ezra Pound.* 2 vols. Berkeley: U of California P, 1980-84.

"Thorez, Maurice." *Webster's New Biographical Dictionary.* 1983 ed.

"Tinkham Calls Col. House 'Un-American'; Demands Inquiry on His War Activities." *New York Times* 7 Feb. 1936, late ed.: 11.

"Tinkham, George H(olden)." *Current Biography.* 1942 ed.

"Tinkham Suggested for President." *Boston Herald* 7 Feb. 1939: 10.

"Tinkham Will Ask End of Peace Pact." *New York Times* 26 Dec. 1935, late ed.: 2.

"To Teach at Notre Dame: Irish and English Economists." *New York Times* 7 Apr. 1935, late ed., sec. 1: 27.

Tolischus, Otto D. "Germany Jubilant." *New York Times* 30 Sep. 1939, late ed.: 1.

_____. "Germany's 'Right' to Colonies Urged: Ribbentrop at the Leipzig Fair Says Return of Territory is Demanded for Trade." *New York Times* 2 Mar. 1937, late ed.: 8.

_____. "Reich Is Shifting Tasks to Industry." *New York Times* 16 May 1958, late ed.: 8.

_____. "Schacht Upholds Nazi Trade Policy." *New York Times* 30 Nov. 1938, late ed.: 16.

"Tugwell, Rexford Guy." *Webster's New Biographical Dictionary.* 1983 ed.

"Two Out, One to Go." *Time* 11 May 1942: 21-22.

"U. S. Rescued Franc in Recent Crisis, Tannery Reveals." *New York Times* 17 June 1935, late ed.: 1, 7.

"Urges Study of Plan for World Exchange." *New York Times* 6 June 1936, late ed.: 22.

"Vandenberg, Arthur Hendrick." *Biographical Directory of the American Congress 1774-1971*. 1971 ed.

"Vanderlip, Frank Arthur." *New Century Cyclopedia of Names*. 1954 ed.

"Vickers' Acquisition: Vickers-Armstrongs Shares." *The Times* (London) 17 July 1935, Royal ed.: 20.

"Villard, Oswald Garrison." *New Century Cyclopedia of Names*. 1954 ed.

"Viscount Templewood Dead; Ex-British Foreign Secretary." *New York Times* 9 May 1959, late ed.: 21.

"Voorhis, Horace Jerry." *Biographical Directory of the American Congress 1774-1971*. 1971 ed.

Walkiewitz, E. P., and Hugh Witemeyer. "Ezra Pound's Contributions to New Mexican Periodicals and His Relationship with Senator Bronson Cutting." *Paideuma* 9 (1980): 441-59.

"Wallace, Henry Agard." *New Century Cyclopedia of Names*. 1954 ed.

"Warburg, James Paul." *Webster's New Biographical Dictionary*. 1983 ed.

"Warren, George Frederick." *New Century Cyclopedia of Names*. 1954 ed.

"Wendel, François de." *New Century Cyolopedia of Names*. 1954 ed.

"Wheeler, Burton Kendall." *Biographical Directory of the American Congress 1774-1971*. 1971 ed.

"Wheeler, Burton Kendall." *Current Biography*. 1941 ed.

"Whitney Receives 5 to 10 Year Term; Court Berates Him." *New York Times* 12 Apr. 1938, late ed.: 1.

Willkie, Wendell. "Political Power." *Atlantic Monthly* 160 (1937): 210-18.

"Zaharoff, Sir Basil." *New Century Cyclopedia of Names*. 1954 ed.

DISCARD